C000054474

UFO SKY PILOTS

Pilots of Peace and Oneness

Grant Cameron

Copyright © 2022 by Grant Cameron

Cover Produced by Matt Lacasse

Editing by Desta Barnabe

Interior Design and Layout by Desta Barnabe

All rights reserved.

No part of this publication may be reproduced, distributed, or transmitted in any form or by any means, including photocopying, recording, or other electronic or mechanical methods, without the prior written permission of the publisher, except in the case of brief quotations embodied in critical reviews and certain other non-commercial uses permitted by copyright law. For permission requests, write to the publisher, addressed "Attention: Permissions Coordinator," at the website below.

Printed and bound in the United States of America

First Printing October 2022

ISBN: 9798359225410

Itsallconnected Publishing

whitehouseufo@gmail.com

www.itsallconnected.weebly.com

www.presidentialufo.com

Contents

Dedicated to Pam DuPuis
Your 2013 story changed everything for me.
We will talk again on the flipside.

Introduction

From my perspective, the future of UFO discourse does, in my opinion, have a future with the burgeoning field of human consciousness...I would say that in the last ten years, there has been a revolution in th focus on consciousness as being primary, so if I had to look for low-hanging fruit for the future of UFO studies, I would probably focus on the impact of these new images of consciousness. Is the UFO phenomenon relevant to these new images of consciousness?
-Colm Kelleher, who managed the day-to-day operations of the AAWSAP Defense Intelligence Agency's investigation of Skinwalker Ranch.

I have encountered several unusual issues in writing this book on such a bizarre topic: conscious flying saucers supposedly visiting the earth and conscious humans interacting with them.

The first one that stands out is that I seem to be the only one with this information, or at least the only person I know who has a steady stream of folks telling me their stories about flying a UFO. I am good at researching and finding supporting references, but I found very few this time.

I examined the John Mack, Budd Hopkins, David Jacobs, and Whitley Strieber material and found only the briefest references. This may have been because the researchers I searched had not asked the question. Perhaps they did not see it as significant?

The weirdest thing about the stories of people flying the craft is that no one in the UFO world seems to care. When I first brought it up to track down the people who responded to the Foundation for Research into Extraterrestrial and Extraordinary experiences, they told me that many different things are reported on the craft.

My reply was that when different people declare that they are flying the craft with their minds, don't you think this is something we should pay attention to? But unfortunately, there was no reply, and there has never been much of a reaction from the UFO community about something that might become the Rosetta stone to figuring out what the hell is going on.

Right or wrong, I wondered if what I call the *UFO Sky Pilots* might be connected to my 2012 noetic experience. Maybe I was now a consciousness magnet that, in some bizarre synchronicity, started linking me to these people.

The fact that so many independent people have described something that would seem nonsensical in the secular-religious worldview indicates that what people are experiencing might be veridical or true evidence. Otherwise, why would someone place something so stupid into the story of their UFO experience?

Some secular believers, who trust only in the Darwinian idea that we are biological robots in a random meaningless universe, don't believe scores of people and their stories about UFOs being a conscious craft. They don't believe the many experiencers who claim to *know* the ship is conscious. Lastly, they would never think the experiencer became "one" with the craft and then used their consciousness to move the craft anywhere in the non-local consciousness that makes up the universe.

These people don't believe this as it would sink their worldview of meaningless materialism. No one wants to admit that most of what they believe is wrong.

The idea that potentially hundreds of people all made up some bizarre story about flying a UFO with their mind is a possibility. Still, it seems that it should be followed with the words, "and the cow jumped over the moon, the little dog laughed to see such fun, and the dish ran away with the spoon." But, of course, both scenarios are equally possible.

Another statement that could be made in contrast to the belief that these experiencers had a collective illusion was first about UFOs and then about flying a conscious craft. The statement came from Terence McKenna, who called such thinking "the limit case for credulity." Terence stated that if someone could believe one of these limited cases, "what is there in the universe that the person can't believe?"

When it comes to illusions, I would say we have to go back to the words of Deepak Chopra, who stated, "everything is an activity inside consciousness." The key word in the sentence is *everything*. In fact, the illusion may be the exact opposite, as most people encountering matrix environments in Near-Death-Experiences, Out-Of-Body Experiences, and lucid dreams will say, "it is more real than the real world."

We often find people claiming absolute knowledge in secular science, even though science theoretically never says anything is proved. For example, science builds models of our universe, which regularly change as new things are discovered. Another example is the atom, which science originally decided was solid and indivisible. Then it was regarded as a positive object with electrons embedded into it like raisins in a plum pudding. The model changed again, and the atom was seen with electrons rising around the nucleus like planets. Then the electron was moving around, but its location was unknown until it was measured.

However, scientists encountering UFO experiencer stories will play with the words and claim, "we know, and you just believe."

Their idea is that anything that can be seen, measured, and duplicated is **real**; anecdotal stories from UFO experiencers are just **beliefs**.

Again, Deepak Chopra and others point out that "everything is an activity inside consciousness." There are no nouns or objects. It is all an active evolving verb.

Princeton physicist John Wheeler put the same observation more scientifically, saying,

> *Recent decades have taught us that physics is a magic window. It shows us the illusion that*

lies behind reality—and the reality that lies behind the illusion. Moreover, its scope is immensely greater than we realized. We are no longer satisfied with insights only into particles, fields of force, geometry, or even space and time. Today we demand of physics some understanding of existence itself.

In another statement, he stated, "The universe does not 'exist, out there' independent of all acts of observation. Instead, it is in some strange sense a participatory universe."

Everything that we think is out there is actually in our minds. Everything is gathered by the body's senses and recreated in our mind with color, shape, taste, smell, and feeling. Without the mind, there is no experience, and as magicians have shown repeatedly, the senses can be fooled to create a world that is an illusion.

We can run tests and create mathematical formulas to explain reality, but these, too, are merely activities inside consciousness. We could be dreaming or hallucinating. How does one tell? The scientist would say numerous people ran the experiment and testified the same result. But how is that different from people claiming to have flown the ship? Both rely on collective experience to determine possible reality.

This "no out there, out there" concept can even be extended to the world of the paranormal. Take, for example, the idea of someone having a near-death experience or out-of-body experience where they find themselves floating above their body.

They may say, "my consciousness was outside of my body. However, I could see my body on the operating table with nurses, doctors, etc."

The reality is that everything is still inside consciousness. The doctors and nurses are in consciousness, but so is the physical body. The body, table, doctors, and nurses are all activities inside the consciousness watching through whatever senses are being used.

The complicated problem of consciousness gets more challenging when we start to look at the evidence of people who reported Near-Death-Experiences, Out-of-Body-Experiences, and sometimes abduction experiences. They find themselves out of their body, looking back at their body.

That leads to the question of who is looking back at the body and how does it see and hear? Does the etheric body reported have physical eyes with retinas and corneas? Does it gather in the light waves and transfer them to the brain? Does the etheric body have a physical brain? Then, where is the perceived reality being projected?

Out-of-body and near-death experiences would then go within and not outside the body. So the entire universe is within, or again as Wheeler says, "there is no out there, out there."

This would fit with the present theories that there is no understanding of the complex problem of consciousness. Where is the mind? Where are the memories? Where are the screen and speakers for the movie we are watching?

Jacques Vallée asked who the observer was when he said:

> *Instead of looking at the screen, I want to turn around and look the other way. Looking the other way, we see a little hole at the top of the wall with some light coming out. So that's where I want to go. I want to steal the key to the projectionist's booth, and then, when everyone has gone some, I want to break in.*

It becomes apparent that the physical interpretation of how senses are collected and experienced starts to fall apart once the NDE, OBE, and abduction material are seriously studied.

It also raises the importance of the research being done in many countries at the moment of training blindfolded children (and some adults) to see. Trainers teach blindfolded children to see color in minutes. Over time, these children can play games, read books, and do a whole host of other things with their blindfolds on, making it apparent that they are not using their physical eyes to see.

Instead, what these kids report sounds strikingly similar to the things written about in NDEs and OBEs. For example, two of the trained children both independently reported that they could hear what sounded like people talking a mile away or that they were able to see things in the future.

The skeptic will reject all this and refuse to look at the evidence or test these children to find out what is really going on. Instead, they resort to assuming that the children are simply guessing.

This attitude is equivalent to someone going down with the Titanic and finding themselves dog-paddling to stay alive. A corner lamp from one of the rooms floats by, and they grab it, hoping it will keep them alive. It will not; similarly, the counter-explanations to the blindfolded children being able to see are useless.

The Mission

One connecting part of the story of flying the craft is that many of these witnesses describe themselves as having a mission connected to their experiences on the ship. Usually, the mission has to do with rescuing the planet from the scourge of nuclear weapons and nuclear power, as detailed in some of the upcoming stories.

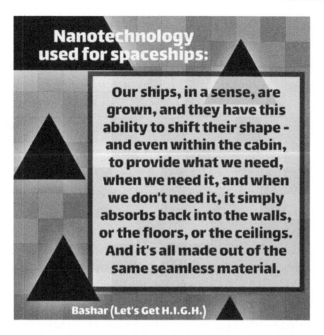

Nanotechnology used for spaceships:

Our ships, in a sense, are grown, and they have this ability to shift their shape - and even within the cabin, to provide what we need, when we need it, and when we don't need it, it simply absorbs back into the walls, or the floors, or the ceilings. And it's all made out of the same seamless material.

Bashar (Let's Get H.I.G.H.)

Some experiencers, like Ron Johnson, were told that his mission was to fly people off the planet at the right time. This mission is strangely reminiscent of the lyrics to the famous song Neil Young sang, which led me to write the book *Tuned-In: The Paranormal World of Music*.

Neil wrote the song "After the Gold Rush" which hinted that we were treating the world like a gold rush, and when the gold is gone, it will become a gold rush, and the saucers will come to move the chosen ones off of the planet.

Well, I dreamed I saw the silver spaceships lying
In the yellow haze of the sun
There were children crying and colors flying
All around, the chosen ones
All in a dream, all in a dream
The loading had begun
Flyin' mother nature's silver seed
To a new home in the sun
Flyin' mother nature's silver seed
To a new home

Consciousness Awakening

Your vision will become clear only when you can look into your own heart. Who looks outside, dreams; who looks inside, awakes.
-Carl Jung

There's a whole other reality that surrounds us that we just simply don't have the ability to see.
-Ex-CIA officer Jim Semivan

I first thought about the role of consciousness within the UFO mystery in 2012 when I had a noetic experience while watching Collin Andrews speak in Phoenix, Arizona. Instantaneously I was "given" three pieces of information regarding research I had already done. The noetic experience put these pieces together in one place, so I could see that they were all related and a possible key to opening the UFO-mystery lock.

The noetic download also indicated that some elements in the government working on the UFO problem had figured out the consciousness connection. However, they may not have known how it worked, but they knew that consciousness was a key component.

The first of the three pieces of information I received was a line from the *Top-Secret UFO Memo* that the Canadian Wilbert Smith wrote to get funding for a government study of flying saucers. This program led to new propulsion development.

Smith wrote that American officials had given him information on what they knew about the flying saucers. These insights included 1) Flying saucers exist, 2) It is the most highly classified subject in the United States, 3) There was a small group headed by scientist and presidential advisor Vannevar Bush to figure out how the saucers worked, 4) The subject was of tremendous significance to the Americans.

Then in the following line, Smith stated that he had been told that other things might be associated with the saucers,

8

such as mental phenomena. The Americans were not doing well in figuring out this part and were willing to talk to the Canadians working on the mental aspect.

The critical thing to note about this is that the memo was written in 1950, just as the modern UFO mystery narrative started. Even the word UFO was not established until 1952. This indicates that officials knew the key to the mystery right from the word GO, but it was held in secrecy or rejected by those wishing for a nuts-and-bolts answer.

The second part of my noetic experience was the words of Dr. Eric Walker. He was the co-developer of the homing torpedo in World War II, was on the Defense Science Board, and was the Chairman of the Board at the Institute for Defense Analysis. This was the top military think tank, where groups like DARPA and the Jason physicists arose. Lastly, Walker was President at Penn State University for 15 years and was president emeritus when a group of UFO researchers worldwide talked to him.

Like the Canadian government memo, Walker indicated the key role of consciousness. He implied that it must be understood to grasp what is really going on in the UFO-mystery search.

In 1990 Walker stated, "What do you know about the 7th sense? Unless you understand, you will not be brought in (to the control group). Very few people understand." It wasn't until this line popped into my head in Phoenix that I suddenly understood what Walker was talking about. He was always talking in riddles, probably because he wanted to speak but could not directly answer questions.

The third piece of the puzzle that popped into my head at that minute was the words of Ben Rich, the Chairman of Lockheed Skunkworks. This organization has always been rumored to be the contractor trying to back engineer the UFO technology.

In 1993, shortly before he died, Rich gave a speech to the engineering alums at UCLA. In the audience was young engineer Jan Harzan, then the head of the Mutual UFO Network (MUFON).

As the lecture ended, Rich suddenly indicated that we had the technology to take ET home. We already had discovered the mistake in the equation. It would not take a lifetime to do.

Harzan had been obsessed with UFOs since a close encounter sighting in his backyard when he was ten years old. As Rich left the building, Harzan raced after him to talk to him. He told Rich that he had always been interested in UFOs and that he and his brother wanted to build one. He asked Rich how they got here and how the propulsion system worked.

Rich turned and asked precisely the same question that Dr. Walker had requested in 1991, "What do you know about ESP?"

Harzan did not expect a question back. Instead, he thought and said, "All things in time and space are connected?"

"That's how it works," replied Rich as he got in his car and drove away.

Later in 2015, another story confirmed that Lockheed Skunkworks knew about the consciousness connection. Tom DeLonge, the former lead singer for Blink-182, had become infatuated with UFOs. Wanting to be involved, he developed a plan to get the message out to the young people he believed were ignoring the messages being put out by the government. He believed with his large Twitter and Instagram accounts, he could get the message out to his young fan base.

In a series of events, DeLonge was invited to talk to Robert Weiss, Executive Vice-President & General Manager at the Skunkworks Advanced Development Programs. DeLonge also told a story that confirmed that the head scientist knew about this consciousness connection to the UFOs. However, evidence indicates that this has not helped them, as there has to be a consciousness interface to the craft, which they do not appear to have. Stories coming from other government insiders indicate that the government has had no success with back engineering the flying saucer because they can't understand how to make the consciousness interace work

It appears that the craft is powered and directed by consciousness which needs a particular experiencer's consciousness to operate. Not just anyone can use their consciousness to turn on the craft.

Tom alleged that during his visit to a Lockheed sensitive compartmented information facility (SCIF), the head scientist asked him how the crafts worked. At that time, DeLonge followed Steven Greer, who constantly talked about the consciousness connection to the UFOs, so DeLonge said *consciousness*.

"Now you are talking," the scientist told him. Tom reported that after this, all the guy wanted to talk about was consciousness for the next 45 minutes.

After receiving this *download*, as I call it, or noetic experience in 2012, I was confident that consciousness was the answer. I did not, however, understand that the answer would be non-local consciousness instead of consciousness. Previously to this experience, I had never thought about the subject. I have joked many times that in 2012, I could not have spelled the word consciousness and couldn't have cared less.

It was not until I had done some research and was giving my first consciousness lecture to the Phoenix MUFON group that I would meet the first of the UFO Pilots. When I first heard the story, I thought it was a joke, but the light came on when I realized that she was telling the truth. I started to realize consciousness was not only necessary, but it could be the key piece to unlocking the mystery.

The Pilots Step Forward

The most substantial evidence for the consciousness connection is the dozens of people independently telling their stories of being on a craft that is alive and that they are allowed to pilot. EVERYONE says it is done with the MIND. There are no exceptions.

The Foundation for Research into Extraterrestrial and Extraordinary surveyed thousands of people who claimed they had contact with non-human intelligence.

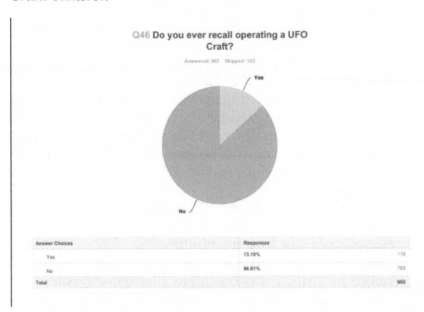

Q46 Do you ever recall operating a UFO Craft?

Answered: 902   Skipped: 532

Answer Choices	Responses	
Yes	13.19%	119
No	86.81%	783
Total		902

According to what science claims to know about reality, the number should have been zero. The modern paradigm asserts that consciousness is nothing more than an epiphenomenon of the brain and that no consciousness outside the brain can control matter, such as flying saucers or anything else.

Some will propose that this is an illusion or screen imaging, but this also does not explain anything. This is just using a word as a placeholder for something someone does not want to believe.

Others will say these stories are anecdotal and are, therefore, useless as they cannot be tested by science, which is the predominant evaluator in the modern world regarding what reality really is.

The facts are that a whole series of people have come forward telling an absurd story. Moreover, they all seem to report the same exact thing, which indicates they are describing something outside of our understanding, which, if taken seriously, could change how we see the world.

When Is A Story Useful Evidence?

Scientists will state that the results of any experiment must be reproducible, measurable, and predictable. Yet, they still believe that there is a world out there, independent of us, that is unchanging and measurable.

I will list other examples later, but a lesson from Skinwalker Ranch shows there may be things that are not unchanging and measurable. Robert Bigelow, who owned the ranch and spent millions studying it, stated that NOTHING ever happened the same way twice.

When they set up cameras hoping to capture an event at a particular spot where something had happened, the intelligence would have the next event be different and just off-camera. Does this mean that the ever-changing phenomenon can't teach us something? Maybe it teaches us that the independent world "out there" that Einstein argued with Bohr about does not exist.

Using the scientific measurement argument, we can take the example of the sun rising and setting each day. It is observable. We can measure its movement across the sky. We can predict almost to the second when it will rise and set and when the equinoxes occur. We can then determine that the sun rotates around the world. Right?

The same can be said for the flat earth. We can put a level anywhere on the planet, and it will show the world is flat. The world looks flat, and we can draw maps of the flat earth that can be used to predict how long it will take from A to B. It is measurable and predictable. So, does that conclude that the world is flat?

I will cite two examples that clearly show there may be many interpretations of what is going on using the same evidence.

We rely on our five senses as the only way to resolve reality; in this way, we box ourselves into a corner. How would the world look if the sun did go around the earth? If the Earth were flat, everything would be solid, and we would be at the center of the universe. Yet, that is precisely the way it looks right now.

Take a look at the science of global warming, genetically modified foods, windmill energy, and or the use of vaccines. How well is the scientific method working in these cases? Does one side "know" and the other just "believe."

We are left in the humbling position that we may not know a damn thing about what is going on, as hinted by many paranormal research observations. It is that 5% of anomalies that some chose to ignore, and others chose to explore, looking for a Nobel Prize.

It is all belief, despite the certainty of some researchers. It may also all be a dream. The ego must take a rest from its quick conclusions. This kind of thing has led to mistake after mistake. It dreamt up the idea of atoms that were solid. That turned out to be wrong. It dreamed up the flat Earth. That appears to be incorrect. The same went for the idea that there was only one galaxy, and that illusion went on until 1929 and was only changed after many bitter debates.

That led to exposing the scientific idea that we were at the center of the Universe or the only intelligent life around. "But where is everybody?" said Fermi in a conversation with Edward Teller, Herbert York, and Emil Konopinski. In 2017 the Pentagon became clear that something was flying around that wasn't from around here. Who is laughing now?

In 1911, science learned it was wrong about atoms being solid. However, it was only at the 1927 Solvay Conference that we started to learn about the observer effect, spooky action at a distance, and many other things that led Einstein to accuse Niels Bohr of trying to drag mysticism into physics.

The attitude that "we know it all" was used on a Max Planck University advisor in 1874 to advise him to stay out of physics as it had all been figured out. Planck continued to study the 5% anomalies, gathered the evidence, won the Nobel Prize, and took a lot of shit for his proposal.

That led him to point out the truth, and this became known as the "science advances one funeral at a time" quote:

A new scientific truth does not triumph by convincing its opponents and making them see the light, but rather because its opponents eventually die, and a new generation grows up that is familiar with it.

The New World Order

In the years since 2017, when the New York Times disclosed that the government does study UFOs, many scientists have been forced to acknowledge that they were wrong after 75 years of scoffing at UFO reports, such as an article in the 1976 *Physics Today Magazine*:

> *The dedicated Ufologists naturally resent the conclusion reached by the late Edward U. Condon, who directed the Air Force Commission study of UFOs at the University of Colorado. Condon's conclusion was that 'UFOs are a dead-end street, a waster of time, [The study] deserves the support of science, not the ridicule it has generally received from the 'believers."*

This does not mean that their God is dead and a new world is rising up. On the contrary, many accept only that the government has acknowledged some unknowns. They doubt there is any new physics, especially if it involves something that counters the belief in materialism.

As Max Planck pointed out over a hundred years ago, scientific ideas don't win over the establishment view, but rather the old believers die off, and new generations will adopt the new concept as they are not challenging.

Therefore, there are many levels of disclosure that we have gone through before we can look at the UFO phenomenon as a whole and determine what is really going on.

One example of this is a 2004 paper that computer scientist Dr. Jacques Vallée wrote and physicist Dr. Eric Davis called *Incommensurability, Orthodoxy and the Physics of High Strangeness: A 6-layer Model for Anomalous Phenomena*[1]

In this paper, the two men pointed out the various levels of the phenomenon based on 30 years of research for Davis and 66 years for Vallée. The six levels they said were involved included:

> *Layer 1 – The physical layer*
> *Layer 2 – Anti-physical*
> *Layer 3 – Psychology of witnesses*
> *Layer 4 – Physiological reactions experienced by witnesses*
> *Layer 5 – Psychic element, as pointed out in parapsychology literature*
> *Layer 6 – Cultural*

The level that this book is focused on is Level 5. It is the most challenging to the belief in a nuts-and-bolts worldview.

Even the UFO community has trouble with the term "psychic," as it sounds, woo-woo, and woo-woo still isn't cool.

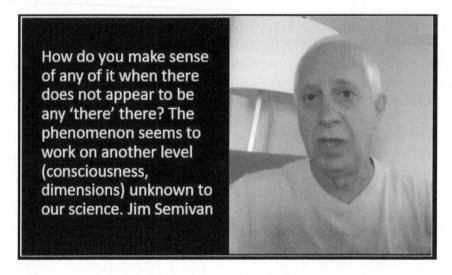

How do you make sense of any of it when there does not appear to be any 'there' there? The phenomenon seems to work on another level (consciousness, dimensions) unknown to our science. Jim Semivan

One example of this is the statement by former CIA official Jim Semivan, after a personal encounter with the intelligence behind the phenomenon and 30 years of serious investigation, that there may be no "there there."

Another example is Dr. Steven Greer's recent report about a person who was in an out-of-body experience or astral projection and had bumped into a flying saucer. The idea was that the astral body and the saucer might be in the same vibration or dimensional space.

I would be willing to bet that only 1-2 % of researchers would accept that story as true. Still, after reading three dozen similar stories in this book, it may be another idea that will take many funerals to become accepted in the zeitgeist.

The Flying Saucer Consciousness History

The consciousness story goes back to the start of the modern UFO mystery, which broke loose in 1947. Already mentioned above is the information provided in 1950 to the director of the Canadian Flying Saucer investigation that mental phenomenon might be part of the mystery. Combine that with the rumor that a telepathic alien survived the 1947 Roswell crash, and you have ideas entirely contrary to what most scientists believe.

Philip Corso

In his controversial book *The Day After Roswell*, Lieutenant-Colonel Philip J. Corso claimed that there was a consciousness interface to the Roswell craft's propulsion.

Corso served on President Eisenhower's National Security Council staff and the sensitive Operations Coordination Board (later known as the "Special Group" or "54/12 Committee", which may have given him access to this probably Top-Secret information.

He claimed to have been allowed to transfer alien technology acquired from the Roswell craft to military contractors through his position with the US Army Staff's Foreign Technology Division.

Corso backed up his claim of a consciousness connection by claiming that the great rocket scientist Dr. Hermann Oberth "suggests we consider the Roswell craft . . . not a spacecraft but a time machine." According to Corso, Oberth speculated, "This was a time/dimensional travel ship that didn't traverse large distances in space. Rather, it 'jumped' from one time/space to another or from one dimension to another and instantly returned to its point of origin."[2]

Corso's alleged that the aliens retrieved from the Roswell crash "used some form of brain-wave control for navigation." But, according to the scientists who examined the artifacts at Norton Air Force Base, California, and Wright Field, Ohio, there were no conventional technological explanations for how the Roswell craft's propulsion system operated:

> *Among the artifacts we retrieved were devices that looked something like headbands... These devices were a very sophisticated mechanism for translating the electrical impulses inside the creatures' brains into specific commands. Perhaps these headband devices comprised the pilot interface of the ship's navigation and propulsion system... The analysts at Wright Field believed that the sensors on the headbands corresponded with points on the multi-lobed alien brain that generated low-frequency waves, so the headbands formed an integral part of the circuit.[3]*

Some may claim that Corso made up his story about being involved with the Roswell crash and later dishing out the hardware to contractors. Still, he seems to have pinpointed the consciousness connection to the craft that would be repeated by many UFO experiencers years later.

Timothy Good

U.K. researcher Timothy Good is widely regarded as one of the world's leading experts on alien phenomena, renowned for his integrity and resolve as a highly-skilled scholar. He has lectured at the Royal Canadian Military Institute, Royal Naval Air Station, the House of Lords All-Party UFO Study Group, the Institute of Medical Laboratory Sciences, and the Oxford and Cambridge Union societies.

He is the author of *Above Top Secret, Alien Contact, Alien Base, Unearthly Disclosure,* and *Need to Know: UFOs, the Military, and Intelligence.*

He mentions the account of Costa Rican Enrique Castillo Rincón, who told his story of UFO contact and claimed that UFOs use a consciousness interface. Rincón claimed that he had contact but no abduction experiences. His account is in *UFOs: A Great New Dawn for Humanity.*[4]

His experience started in Costa Rica in June 1963, coincidently just as President John Kennedy was about to visit the country. Rincón was employed by the maintenance department of the Costa Rican Institute of Electricity (ICE).

At the same time, there were eruptions from one of its largest volcanoes on the island, Irazú. Rincón and some associates were monitoring the situation. During that operation, they spotted some crafts:

> *Two craft hovered together, stationary, at an altitude of some 300 meters above the crater. The object closest to us suddenly dropped a few meters in a straight line, stopped abruptly, and then started falling slowly, gently swaying from side to side, like a dead leaf falling from a tree. It finally 'parked' three meters above the surface of the volcano's crater, about 60 meters from us.*
>
> *This 'vehicle' was lenticular in shape, about 45 meters in diameter, and 12 meters high. A series of windows emitting blue light was visible around its diameter. It had a well-proportioned, greenish dome seamlessly joined to the main body, which was smooth and the color of lead. When the two machines approached, they looked orange or reddish in color, but when they stopped, they lost that hue. Totally conscious of everything around us, with our senses more alert than ever, but at the same time perplexed and immobilized, we feared for the worst. [Then] the periscope retracted, the door closed, and after a fraction of a second, the craft lifted up a few*

meters as if it were falling upwards; then it tilted slightly and shot off into infinity at a fantastic speed. The second ship followed silently, leaving behind a multi-colored trail, first white, then orange, then reddish, changing to strong blue, and finally fading into violet. The stupendous speed made the craft look oval rather than round. As suddenly as they had appeared a few minutes earlier, they were gone, and we saw them no more. 5

Soon after, Rincón became ill and went to the hospital. When he recovered, he started a UFO study group and was down the rabbit hole. He moved from country to country, and the phenomenon followed him.

As a part of his encounters on the ship, he was shown the propulsion system:

In the innards of the ship, a group of three great diamonds or crystals rotated slowly around a vertical shaft extending from ceiling to floor, which also turned in the opposite direction. The colors and shades of the shaft surface were like a kaleidoscope of pure crystal...

*'Those are crystals, not diamonds,' explained the commander. 'We call them 'memory crystals'; they are programmable and receive information from the 'main transducer' [the rotating shaft]. We also call them 'living crystals.'*6

The system exhibited a connection between the craft and the people piloting the craft. Twelve members of the crew appeared, and twelve dentist-like-chairs appeared out of the floor. Then:

From the ceiling dropped 12 helmets, similar to motorcycle helmets, which descended onto the heads of each of the crew members as soon as they sat in their chairs. The four with the different uniforms sat precisely equidistant. They held hands in 'padlock fashion,' each one holding the arm of the next until the circle was complete . . . This ritual lasted perhaps one minute; then the helmets retracted up into the ceiling, the company stood up and released each other's hands, and the chairs collapsed into the floor . . . They said that I had seen them liberate their mental energy to the transducer, where it would be converted into flight energy![7]

The Early Contactees

One of the other claims Corso made was that hand panels were touched, which flew the craft.

This is supported in a way by some six-finger panels related to the infamous 1995 Alien Autopsy film. Unfortunately, this picture did not appear in the film.[8]

In the year 2000, Ray Santilli openly explained that the image came from a badly damaged piece of the film they couldn't use, but this image from it was copied onto a "slide" and used for publicity.

Timothy Good reported that he talked to one of the early contactees and had been told a similar thing:

> *Desmond Leslie, co-author of 'Flying Saucers Have Landed,' written with George Adamski, the American contactee, told me that in the early 1960s, Adamski had revealed to him in strict confidence that the spacecraft he flew in was operated by 'mental control...' 'It was a small platinum gadget fixed to the forehead,' said Desmond. 'George drew for my children pictures of these handprint things, similar to those described in Corso's book.'*[9]

Don Schmitt

Don Schmitt has been one of the key researchers investigating the Roswell crash, which would have exhibited whatever technology the craft had. However, it appears from what most researchers say that those details are still safely protected behind many levels of security.

It leaves researchers with very little except speculation. When I asked Don what they had discovered about how the craft flies from the witnesses he had encountered, he stated that he had not gathered much solid evidence.

When asked about this consciousness connection to the craft, Schmitt was kind enough to share with me the thinking he and others working on the Roswell crash had done over the years. However, he warned that it was mostly speculation:

> *Obviously, this is mere speculation on our part but is based on sound rationing and eyewitness testimony. As early as 1994, we were already questioning the possibility of thought projection as the means of piloting the Roswell craft. It was about ten years later that we finally got the former 393rd Bomb Sqd. Flight engineer Sgt. William Ennis to admit specific items about the nature of the craft.*

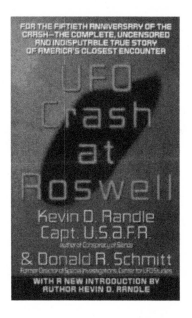
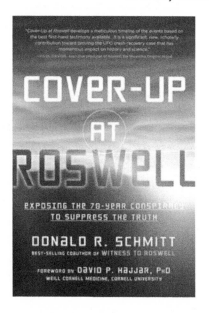

What I will never forget is when he placed his hand on my shoulder and said, 'Don, before I go, you have to find out how that damn thing flew. It didn't have a moving part on it.' We had heard this before - That the craft was absent any propulsion and clearly no engine of any design. So, once again, we returned to the question of thought projection. The pilot becomes one with the ship and mentally commands it. We have recently suggested that the very 'memory material' described by so many witnesses was the actual propulsion. This would also enable it to morph and take on different shapes and dimensions as it maneuvered through the air. All speculation at this juncture but nonetheless fascinating to envision. Hopefully, someday we will see this all become fact.

Betty Andreasson, an experiencer who has had extensive and direct contact since the 1940s, reported something that backed up the Ennis statement that "it didn't have a moving part on it."

During one of her UFO encounters, she moved around in a transparent orb object with no motor or anything else that would drive it. This is what Andreasson reported:

> *The being escorted me into another room where a clear, bubble-like orb waited in the corner. I was told to step into it. When I entered, it did not feel solid. I walked right through it. The separation between the room and the orb seemed not to exist. I sat down in the center of the orb, and it shot out of the craft with me in it. It was like I was moving along in mid-air within a transparent ball of light. I could see the tops of the trees as the orb started to drop downward. As the orb drew level with some trees, I could see our trailer.*

Experiencer Chris Bledsoe also had the experience of being on a transparent, orb-like craft that did not appear to have any visible means of propulsion.

In 2007, during his UFO awakening experience along the Cape Fear River, he disappeared for 4.5 hours. Four other witnesses supported this claim.

During the 4.5 hours, Chris was taken to Egypt, where he flew over the pyramids. He was told about the connection between what was happening to him and ancient Egypt.

I wrote Chris and asked if he had seen any engine or propulsion system in the object he was moving around in. He replied:

> *Nothing. I was standing in a round room with walls, but you couldn't see them.*
>
> *I was standing on a sheet of glass, 1000 feet up, and my view was the three pyramids and the sphynx facing away from me.*
>
> *Also, in 1971 I was shot point-blank in the back (accidentally with a shotgun by a boy he was hunting with). In that near-death experience, the one thing I remember is that I left earth in a clear orb. Clear from the inside. I have*

maintained this for 50 years. Everyone is now talking orbs instead of flying saucers.

Other Researchers

As pointed out earlier, there is very little information put out by researchers that would confirm or deny the stories told by experiencers about flying the craft. This means that people reporting the flying stories could not have pickup up the story from a book. Therefore, there were no books with such stories.

John Mack, a professor at Harvard, wrote two books on alien abduction and the clients he dealt with. Only in one brief case could I find any reference to the conscious craft and people flying it. Mack mentioned that one person said he thought the ship had some kind of consciousness to it.

Like Mack, David Jacobs is a researcher academic at Temple University who worked with many people who claimed they were on craft. He mentioned people being trained onboard the craft in his book *The Threat:*

> *I was also puzzled about why abductees were subjected to strange staging and testing procedures in which they acted out a scenario with aliens or found that they could operate complex devices or perform tasks they do not remember having learned. These procedures seemed unrelated to the breeding program.*

Jacobs rarely talked about conscious crafts seeing the situation more like aliens who were trying to take over the world and who could mess with people's minds and keep them cooperating with the overall invasion plan.

However, he told one story about a woman who was allowed to fly the craft. She stood in her nightgown at a panel with strange hieroglyphic characters. Behind the panel was a window looking out. She could see a grey alien on the ground below being chased by some human in the window.

A grey being stood to her right and looked out the window. She was told she was to maneuver the craft by touching the symbols and rescue the alien. She could only remember one of the symbols but said there were many different ones. At first, she did not believe she could do it, but she suddenly seemed to know what to do as the tension increased. Finally, he put her hand over the one symbol hovering the craft over the stranded alien was, and the rescue took place.

Reading through these stories, you will notice that most witnesses are not touching anything; they only use their minds. In this case, however, the woman was hovering her hand over a symbol to fly the ship.

In the drawing she did for Jacobs, she wrote, "I believe this was all a staging."

The Evidence

Almost three dozen witnesses provide the evidence in this book. These witnesses all had the experience of being on a craft associated with UFO intelligence. They became one with the ship and used their minds to move the craft around. There were no time/space restrictions on where they could go.

The following accounts are anecdotal evidence of an incredible story that makes no sense. However, they are anecdotal evidence, like the UFO sightings that people have reported over the last 75 years, and it appears that those rejected tales will turn out to be true.

In December 2017, *The New York Times* ran a front-page story disclosing the reality of UAPs. It turned out that the millions of people around the globe who had been reporting witnessing UFOs were correct. The same would apply to all the UFO metals that people have reported falling out of the sky. Researchers have discovered they are not typical metals and that the absurd stories of molten metal or crashing ships are probably genuine encounters.

Dr. Garry Nolan is a Stanford University School of Medicine professor who researches microbiology, immunology, and bio-computation. He also analyzes UFO artifacts, materials, and reports of UFO encounters. He commented once on UFO data that I think applies to these flying-the-ship reports.

> *There's still raw data, and you have to listen once you start to hear the same story again and again. Then you have to say, well, there might be something to it.*[10]

What is interesting to note is that the stories are never exactly the same, but the fundamental story is the same. I think this will be an essential point that will tie into how we perceive reality.

Modern science is still embedded in Einstein's world, where the moon is still there when we are not looking at it. In other words, there is a world out there that is independent of us. It is unchanging and can be measured. That is the real and only reality.

The "flying-the-ship stories" differ in how the witnesses interacted with the craft. One person put his hand on a beehive object in the middle of the room. Some put their hand on a round ball on the console. Some put their hand over the ball but didn't touch it. Some put their hands on a flat console. Some put their fingers in holes in the arm of a chair. I don't think that any two are the same.

This would indicate many different crafts, and we have yet to match up two people who flew the same craft. It could also mean a plastic nature to the experience that lets people have different experiences but the same principle, and we have failed to notice. Some supporting evidence includes:

- Dr. Kit Green, a former CIA official who has looked at UFO data for decades, said, "For some witnesses, the appearance between what is seen and what really is will somehow become fully distorted, and in most cases unrecognizable. Also, it is as if from a certain distance, or point of view concerning what is being perceived, a witness will interpret the event or experience based on his or her own preconceived views and beliefs."
- One of the critical paranormal researchers of the 20th century, John Keel, said, "The UFO phenomena are frequently reflective. The practical manifestations seem to be deliberatively tailored and adjusted to the individual beliefs and mental attitudes of the witnesses. Both the objects and occupants appear to be able to adopt a magnitude of forms, and the contactees are usually given information which conforms to their own beliefs...the witnesses are not the perpetrators of these hoaxes but are merely the victims."

- Brandon Fugal, the present owner of Skinwalker Ranch, said, "I have noticed on a number of occasions people who bring negativity to the ranch, that bring a spirit of contention or negativity, end up experiencing negativity. The ranch seems to be reflexive, at least to respond in a very dynamic way to the spirituality or psychology of those who enter."
- People talk a lot about the different aliens, in particular the greys. The greys first appeared in July 1961 to Nancy Tremaine and her girlfriend. People tend to assume that all aliens are the same. As an experiment, I took about 20 drawings made of greys done by the witnesses and found no two were the same. Some of the drawings had huge differences. The core story was there, but there was an element that indicated the witness were part of what was being seen.
- I wrote a book on UFO triangles called, *Triangles, Aliens and Messages* and suddenly realized the same problem. When you started comparing the accounts, there were no two triangle-shaped UFOs that seemed to be the exact same. Sometimes the lighting was different, the size was different, some were triangles, and some were boomerangs.
- The reports on UFOs show even more dramatic differences in the lights, sizes, windows, colors, etc. For example, in the two sightings I had in 1975, the object changed as I watched it. This happened at least twice.
- At the Skinwalker Ranch, researchers said they had an impossible task researching the paranormal events because nothing ever happened the same way twice. Again, there is an underlying story of paranormal activity but a very plastic environment where nothing shows itself the same way twice.
- A parallel phenomenon occurs during the dream state and directly hints that we are part of what we see. I have had one repeating dream at least a dozen times. The dream is backed with emotion, and I wake up completely wound up. Like the UFO, grey, or flying the ship, the core message of the dream is exactly the same,

but one element changes every time. The last time it happened, I laughed as I was floored at how my higher self (or whoever is directing the dream) could change the plot every time to tell the whole story. I fall for it every time. I am not a Hollywood scriptwriter; therefore, I am stunned that the whole dream is so dramatic and real, yet just a rerun of an old dream. No two of these dreams have ever been the same. (I wrote this, and I had the dream the next night. Same theme and message but a new plotline that I fell for hook, line, and sinker.)

The investigation has led me to believe that this flying-the-ship has an underlying message, but the whole thing is as individual as dreams.

I mention this because I think this is also a characteristic of the UFO phenomena. Scientists and researchers are looking for a common pattern. They figure that if they get enough data, there will be a real world and an unchangeable object. I have my doubts.

The Witnesses

Jake Crowder
@volfan3178

Replying to @slide999 @GrantCameron and 4 others

Think of it like how you use your arms and legs, but you move the craft like that.

1:03 PM · May 27, 2022 · Twitter Web App

I have a list of about 50 people who have reported having flown a UFO. I believe that I am the only one who has compiled these testimonies and the only person who has put them out for public consumption. Therefore, the people telling me about flying the craft could not have read it in a book or heard about it from another person.

More importantly, if someone believes 50 people could all come out simultaneously with some incredible story, that person would fit into the *limit case for credulity* category. This states that if you believe the mass illusion explanation, what in the world is there that you wouldn't believe?

None of the witnesses has sold their flying story. None have even pushed to tell it. Yet, it may be the most essential UFO evidence ever recorded. It is the anomaly of all anomalies. If the observations are accurate, we have some critically important things to learn about consciousness and reality.

There have been a few brief references to the conscious craft and the experiencers who have been allowed to pilot these UFO vehicles:

- In Helmut Lammer's book *MILABS* – "The being was telepathically instructing her how to maneuver around objects while navigating. The Gray told her that the craft could 'sense' objects and maneuver around them."
- From the testimony of one experiencer to MILAB/Abductee researcher Melinda Leslie - "I willed the ship with thought."
- From another testimony of one experiencer to MILAB/Abductee researcher Melinda Leslie - "The ship is alive, you just think it."
- From another testimony of one experiencer to MILAB/Abductee researcher Melinda Leslie - "The ship did what I thought. I did it with feeling like it was alive."
- Mary Rodwell is an Australian UFO researcher and regressionist who has amassed thousands of cases of experiencer's stories. I asked whether she has encountered cases of people claiming to have flown the craft; she replied, "Yes, many have said they are 'taught ' to fly craft even as children."

Pam DuPuis

When the final history is written on the truth behind the UFO phenomena, Pam DePuis's name will be front and center. I firmly believe that consciousness is key to understanding what is going on. The stories regarding flying the ship clearly show significant evidence that validates the role of consciousness in the UFO game.

Many more experiencers have talked about this flight via consciousness, even before Pam. For example, in 2007, Jim Sparks said that he observed "thought-activated technology" and that the aliens he encountered could "command their machines with thought."

David Adair had a very controversial story about launching a nuclear-fusion electromagnetic containment engine he had built in the Area 51 area of Nevada when he was 17 years old. It was launched from the White Sands missile range. When they took him there so they could view his rocket, black-suited, government-type men showed him an engine in one of the lower levels below the base. The engine appeared to be damaged with a hole in it. When they asked him to evaluate what had happened, he suddenly believed after touching it that the engine was alive and that it could only be controlled telepathically. He called it *advanced symbiotic technology.* Adair was telling this story many decades ago.

Pam's story, however, woke me up and linked to my noetic experience months earlier. In that encounter, I realized consciousness was the key to understanding the UFO story I had been chasing since 1975.

Here is the story that Pam told the Winnipeg UFO group from a hospice when she was near the end of a long road with cancer. She started by recalling her first memory: being in a field with grass over her head at just over two years of age, knowing she was in trouble because her friends (ETs) had dropped her off at the wrong place. There were a bunch of military boots around her, and she was on a military base. Her stepfather, who had three degrees from the University of Chicago, was in his 50s when the courts awarded Pam and her brother to the family. Her father was a pilot in World War II.

Pam said her father knew what was happening to her as he would ask her about her dreams, and she would have marks on her body or sand and grass in the bed. Sometimes she said she would wake up to find her pajamas were inside out and backward; this is not uncommon with UFO experiencers.

Note on the transcript. We had trouble taping the session, so the following transcript is the only interview Pam ever gave, except for one two-hour interview done with researcher Paul Davids which was never made public.

> *Between 2 and 3 years old, I was brought up onto a ship. There were a lot of other children, maybe 10 or 12. We sat in a circle, and they would put a ball in the middle of the circle, and we would have to move the ball to the other children without touching it. We would have to do it with our minds.*

That did not seem unusual because that is what we did. I was surprised later to find out that every kid didn't have that experience and that they could not do that.

They started there, and they trained our minds, and I got better as time went on. My brother was adopted by me. That's how I can time this. He was one year and ten months younger than I was, and he was an infant at the time... we both had the same experiences, but we were never placed on the ship at the same time, but when we came back, we would play games – mind games. One would think of something, and the other would have to say what it was. We would trade off and take turns. That was just a continuation of the training. It was always a game; it was always fun.

There was never anything frightening. People were always more scary to me than aliens were.

During childhood, there were a lot of painful surgeries. Things were done that hurt a great deal, but it was a positive thing. When I was adopted, the doctors told my parents I would die before I was four. I had kidney failure, and that was a death sentence at that time. Obviously, they (ETs) did something with the kidneys. I don't know what. I turned out fine, and there were never any problems. I had all sorts of physical and mental help.

There were all sorts of things that were going on in training.

Then when I reached my teens, it had to change a bit. I guess kids become rebellious anyway. I didn't like the idea that I had no choice. I got stubborn. I had a few lessons that were a little painful.

I got older and then was introduced to the ships in my teens. First, it was the crude ones. The head pieces were large metal and cumbersome (this flight aid is what people like Corso were claiming for the Roswell time period- see above) with things that fit over the head.

Later, they were small and not even noticeable on your head. A few years after, there was nothing to directly connect to the ship. That worked out well, and I was sent on all kinds of missions and things to do. So was my brother.

Then in my early thirties, I got to be a part of the growing and building products of the ships. It was identified almost in printing. I imprinted on it, and it imprinted on me. It became unified.

Also, at that time, the vision. Space is like being in the water. It is actually that dense. It is not empty at all, but you need a different set of eyes. That is the best way I can explain it. That came through your ship. You can see brilliant colors, lines, energies, and all sorts of things. So that was pretty much the development.

Since I was a child, there was always information being put in. There was teaching. There was training.

I had four ships that I used. One, of course, was always the favorite, and there was a fifth one that was just coming out. I honestly don't know how that one turned out. It wasn't built yet. So, that is how I got around.

It is a very difficult thing to describe because there are no words for that experience (flying the craft). The nearest thing that I could say is that we are functioning as one. It senses and knows, and I sense and know what it is experiencing. What it is thinking, and what is going to be happening.

In some areas, the ship takes over more of the brain work, and in other areas, I do. So, there is a trust relationship there. I give up some, and it gives up some, but the unified is greater than the two separate.

(Asked what job she does with craft) One is to patrol areas. In patrolling space, you could take in a whole section of space that has many, many solar systems within it. You watch boundaries and natural disasters that happen, and then you become a rescue ship. You can also send out alerts and warnings for others to help.

The ships that strictly do perimeters appear as very small ships that are always visible. However, if more is needed, the rest of the ship is in a different space but is connected.

It is very difficult to explain this. You can't see it. If it is needed, it can come into this space, but they don't drag a whole huge ship through this space; 90% of it is not in this space. 90% of it is in the other space. There is a barrier there, but that barrier is easily opened. It is like a sliding door that can open two ways. That is kind of the sense you get.

The crafts can be huge. The largest craft is like three times the size of our solar system. It is divided into areas. Each area has different life forms, but they are all within this giant ship. They are protected.

I don't know if that kind of ship is supposed to be like an ark where they want to preserve these species. I don't know if it was a disaster or a refuge until somewhere else can be found. I don't know exactly what that is. I have been on that ship a couple of times. I have been through a couple of different habitats.

One of the things people wanted to know was about the crystal city, which Pam said was the most beautiful place she had ever flown to. She described what it was like:

I'll try and describe it. The entrance I always take in is over a bridge. The bridge is all crystal. Once you cross that bridge and get into the rest of the city, there is no up or down. You can be upside down walking on a crystal pathway, and right above you, people's feet are exactly where your feet are. It is very disorienting at first.

It is very heavily populated, but the beings that are the population of that city have the capability of healing. They are very peaceful beings. Because it is crystal, you can see through it partly. If you get more walls, it becomes denser, so you can only see so far. The beings are thin and tall. You can't see their faces. They do show their faces, but I can't grasp it.

There are many, many beings there so that the city can seem pretty populated, but they are not the natives of the city. They are the ones that open it up and allow you in or don't allow you.

So, you should ask Stacey (Wright). I took a group of people on a trip there with permission. I had to get permission first. One evening we met at Stacey's house. I believe there were seven of us. We went to the crystal city.

When I spoke with Stacey, she described the event as astral traveling with Pam. Stacey ended up in a crystal cave, one woman, Stacey recalled, ended up underwater, and some of those involved had moved, so she couldn't get their version of what they witnessed.

This raises the question of how physical abduction experiences are conducted or any other mystical experience. No one ever witnessed anyone being abducted, and yet there is no doubt that an actual event is taking place. Most abductees describe the event as a dream, matrix reality, or Out-of-Body experience. Eighty percent of all people polled who have dealt with non-human intelligence say they have had an OBE.

Is it true, as Nobel Laureate and father of quantum mechanics, Max Planck said, "As a man who has devoted his whole life to the most clearheaded science, to the study of matter, I can tell you as a result of my research about the atoms this much: There is no matter as such!"

This idea of solipsism: a theory holding that the self can know nothing but its own modifications and that the self is the only existent thing, is discussed in the conclusion. If, for example, there is no time and space, can there be physical planets far away, out in space? Pam continued:

> *I had to ask permission, and it took a couple of months.*
>
> *It may not be so easy to love an 8-9 foot praying mantis; however, the love should be the same. The praying mantis happened to be the nurse made for the young children on the ship I was on. The small greys and there were dark blue guys in shawls. The small greys did the work, so in the shadow, peeking around a corner, or staying back, was the praying mantis. Obviously, she had the run of the ship. She was the intelligence but also a great love and protector. There are three levels of greys. There are the small guys who are very quick. They scoot around a lot. There are ones that are a little taller at 4-5 feet, and then there are the tall greys that are more the scientists. The tall ones and the short ones are very detached. The mediums ones are used alongside the beds that people are being surgically altered on.*
>
> *There are many species of reptilians. The one that I am familiar with is very sensual, very sexual. They are very open. They have families that accept you, which is bizarre, but they do. Then there are the reptilians that are, I don't want to say, more negative. They are far more aggressive. Work has been done on them as far as genetics to get rid of this aggression, but they couldn't do it. They altered them so much that they were not themselves anymore.*

You will see them, but they are never alone. They are usually with other species. They will be with other reptilians, and there are usually a couple on board a ship. They are super intelligent. It is just like a flaw in their genetic makeup. Then other reptilians are very shy, reclusive, and intelligent.

I would say that I know of fifty-two different types, but my first-hand experience over the years on a regular basis, on a weekly or daily basis, has been about five. The others I have seen and crisscrossed with but no real interaction. A more encompassing life of intelligent life, I am probably more forgiving., because the difference between human races can be as different as between alien species...

I was utilized by that group for a couple of years. As far and near as I can explain, I was an ambassador. Information was put into my head, and then I was sent to another species to relay that information. The reason that I was used in this was that I started so young and saw so many species that I had no repulsion or fear. No matter what they looked like, I understood. They are intelligent beings. They happen to look that way, and we look this way.

Also, I had started so young that they could dump information into me... it was everything that they thought about, felt, or experience... I transfer it to whatever species or group that they send me to. I don't even know what it is until I get there, and it comes out.

Sometimes people want more, but they aren't ready. They can become angry, but there's a problem with giving something to someone before they are ready. They have not made the mistakes that led to the discovery of this, and that can be disastrous. It is not out of cruelty or snobbery or anything else. People will ask, 'why

41

don't they show themselves?' Because not everyone is ready. Often you can be ready and don't even realize you are ready. You don't even think about it.

Sometimes aliens will want you with your body to interact with the ship, and sometimes they don't want your body. They just want you. When you are out of your body, those being are just as real. They just don't have a corporal body. As a species, we are not up to being nose-to-nose with them on everything, their knowledge, their spirituality, and their capabilities, but we do interact.

People have the same capability. However, they have not learned to tap it or haven't opened up yet. Don't have the years, decades, or millennium to know.

You don't have to be afraid. They are not going to hurt you. They could have done that long ago. They will give you something or teach you something... as long as you are open and relaxed, and welcoming, I think you will be okay. Don't worry about it. You cannot do anything about it anyway, so enjoy it.

Asked about how long the experiences lasted, Pam got into time.

That is a question I can't really answer because it is never in the same place. It is never in the same place in relation to where you are or in the same place in relation to it. When you travel, you get there almost instantly because you sense or feel where they are. It is like an invisible rubber band.

As soon as you hook on, bam, and there you are. So, where it is, is immaterial. It could be anywhere, so that is never a real big question.

They do have a sense of humor, but it is very juvenile, like the kindergarten of 1st grade. One time I was washing dishes, and there was a grey standing there in my kitchen. I said, 'Hi.' I then turned around and thought, 'what the heck?' I turned back around, and he was gone. That was supposed to be funny.

Your stuff disappears. Your socks, your underwear. It will be gone for a week or two or a couple of days, and then it will show up right back in the middle of the living room table.

All life comes from One God. That is the source, and they (the beings) all know that.

Chris Bledsoe, North Carolina

You become a part of that machine, that metal, that ship. It almost has, like, a soul to it. The craft does. It maybe becomes you into the machine somehow. It is very intelligent.
- Chris Bledsoe talks about flying the craft.

Chris Bledsoe was a North Carolina contractor and businessman with a commercial pilot's license. He is also a UFO experiencer who had an awakening in January 2007 along the Cape Fear River with four other witnesses. He alone was taken onto the craft, where he was kept for 4.5 hours. During that time, he was shown many things, including the great pyramids in Egypt.

He witnessed four 7-foot-tall bluish-green beings on the ship that he would encounter again in the coming years, including two incidents where the beings (now appearing as beings of light) took him to a meeting with what seemed to be a woman in light – the Universal divine feminine.

While onboard the ship, Bledsoe was allowed to fly the craft. When I heard that he had flown the craft, I stopped him and said I would contact him on Skype so that I could record the whole conversation. I wanted him to start from the beginning and continue until the end.

Chris Bledsoe told me in that conversation about how to fly a craft. It matches up perfectly with what the other dozens of experiencers told me about flying the craft.

> *When I walked up to the craft from the outside, is shaped like an egg, and it was faceted but in the shape of a beehive. I'm looking at the outside of the craft. The skin - that's what the skin appears like a form. Real little, tiny honeycombs. As this craft becomes alive, these little, tiny honeycombs expand, and the little ones turn into big ones.*
>
> *Okay, so, entering into the craft, there's this round area towards the front, and there's this pedestal, and it's sort of like a raised area near this console. It's like a pedestal, and on top of it, there is a beehive.*

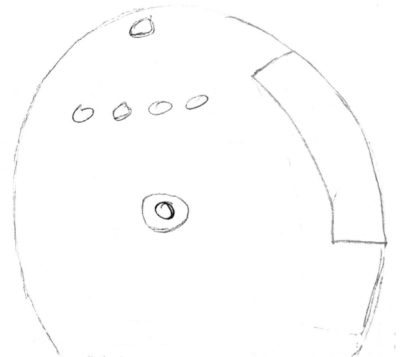

Figure 1 The inside of Chris's craft. Elevated beehive in the middle. Four beings in front of it. Chris is at the top. Panelboard along the right side.

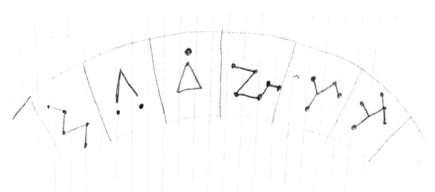

Figure 2 Panel inside craft with lit-up symbols on it seen by Chris.

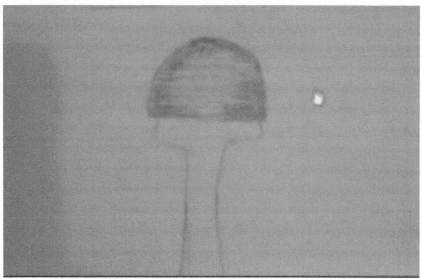

*Figure 3 Pedestal with a beehive-type object that Chris put his hand on.
Drawing by Chris Bledsoe*

It would be half of a beehive. Have of a basketball-size, that size, but not quite round. It's a kind of black, carbon-fiber texture on the outside but in the shape of a honeycomb. Everything is like a honeycomb-like but micro tiny. When I lay my hand on it - they said to lay my hands on it. When I did this, where my hand was (on the beehive) turned into this deep purple-violet color.

Then it began to change; it went through the purples and blues into the green and then got to this aqua-like aquamarine color. The whole thing lit up this pedestal, and it all happened in a very quick manner. I just put my hand on it and pulled away. It cycles colors. Boom! That lights up in the inside of the craft is beginning to light up.

Then from the inside of the craft, I started to see the same kind of texture as what was on the outside of the craft. Millions of tiny little honeycombs started to glow like little LED dots. That's how I would describe them. They were tiny. I am looking at them on a small scale, but then they begin to rotate. Each one is like a mechanical gear.

You see it as a connection to the craft. The craft becomes alive and turns into this huge geometric honeycomb shape. All the little ones are going, and now they are great and big.

Then, after all that startup process happens in seconds, really. It has become a part of me. If I look at something and I want to be there, that's where we go. It leads you. It guides you. It's with you.

I never saw a stick that you drove. It's always been just a stop thought. I had the greatest time going down the river just shouting. I can see out, sitting cross-legged on the floor, looking through the front of the craft. It's as clear as glass. I'm right down on top of the water, just screaming down the river. I went through the connection process. It's surreal. Everything all happens. The sounds, everything happens very quickly.

You become a part of that machine, that metal, that ship. It almost has a soul to it. The craft does. It maybe becomes you into the machine somehow. It is very intelligent.

Ron Johnson, Utah

> Wow, and we were just sitting there, and I
> watching. It was awesome. I asked him. I
> "what am I supposed to do?"
> He says, "It's all inside you. All you have to
> think and the ship will respond to
> ever you want to do."
> I said, "I'd like to go out in the deep space
> see the Milky Way galaxy from a
> nce..."
> It only took maybe a second or so and all
> sudden, we come to a stop way out in
> e somewhere and I'm looking at the Milky
> galaxy.
> ount of UFO Experiencer Ron Johnson

Ron Johnson is a lifelong experiencer from Price, Utah. He has journaled his numerous contacts since the 1960s. These experiences included hybrid-related events, healings, and showing him technology.

> *They were showing me technology. It's like one time they were showing me how to convert a gasoline engine to run on free energy. The only trouble is I can't remember it.*
>
> *You know, at the time, it seems so easy. So, then they showed me a device that allowed me to dimension hop or transcend the different dimensions. They said they have to do that, you know, traveling the vast distance distances that they do. When I flew the ship, it had this machine on it that they showed me here like six months prior in another visitation.*

Ron had a very clear recollection of the time they let him fly the craft. They told him that this was part of his life mission. Ron has told me the story many times on my whitehouseufo YouTube channel, but here is the account he put on his Facebook site.

> *I was face-to-face with Elbe. Our noses were almost touching each other, and it was like he was downloading information into me. There was a real strong feeling of g-force, like I was moving and accelerating real fast.*
>
> *Then all of a sudden, it ended, and I found myself in this cubicle that was up on the ceiling of this big huge, what looked like a big room. There were probably 20 other cubicles up there, and there was a human person in each one of them. I'm in there, and I'm looking down below, and I can see these entities walking around down there, and then pretty soon, one I'm in slowly goes down to the floor, and it opens up. I stepped out and asked them, "Where am I?'*
>
> *He told me that I was on their ship and that it was time for me to find out why I'm going through all this. That's when he told me I was programmed to fly this ship from birth. He stated that it was this ship.*
>
> *He stated you and thousands of others like you would be transporting people to another dimensional earth. I don't know if that's the case; I'm assuming it's another earth and a different, maybe a parallel dimension. I have not sure, but I'm assuming that's what it is.*

I asked Ron if he felt he had been programmed before birth and if this was part of his mission here:

> *I feel like they were. But it's weird because I feel like they're my family, not my family that I have here on earth.*
>
> *I felt at home with them now, and as I said, these beings, all the encounters I've had with them, were very, very positive. The first ones were a little scary...*

After he told me what my purpose was on earth - to fly these to fly this ship to transport the people, he took me over to this big chair, and he had me sit in it.

I'm looking around this ship. It was beautiful inside. It was a room itself that I was in where there was this where the control panel was, where he operated the ship from. It was probably; I'm going to guess, 20- 25 feet high. And the front came to not a sharp point but kind of a rounded point.

It looked like it was made from a real shiny, either black plastic or possibly a black ceramic material. It was very, very shiny and very smooth.

I remember I was looking around everywhere. There were no seams – nothing. It looked like the whole entire ship was injected – injected molding.

I sat down. He had me sit down in the chair and a control panel. It must have been about three feet long and a foot high. It almost looked virtual. It was in the air hanging in front of me, and these symbols would start appearing on this panel.

Now before I did anything, there was in the armrest there were holes on both armrests, a deep impression. He told me that I needed to put my fingers in those holes. He told me to put my arms in the depression on the armrests, and so I did.

What was weird was looking at the seat I had sat in; it didn't look very comfortable. It was comfortable. It fit me perfectly.

As soon as I put my arms and my fingers in those depressions, the whole front of the ship just opened up, and I could look outside. I can see outside into space. The earth was a little ball off in the distance.

Wow, and we were just sitting there, and I was watching. It was awesome. I asked him, I said. 'What am I supposed to do?'

He says, 'It's all inside you; all you have to do is think in the ship will respond to whatever you want to do.'

I said, 'I'd like to go out into the deep space and see the Milky Way galaxy from a distance.'

'Okay,' he says. 'Before we go, I want I want to warn you you're gonna feel g-force right at the very first until we start to transcend the dimensions.'

He also says, 'up until that time, it's going to be very uncomfortable for you.'

So okay, and so I thought, you know, let's go. I want to see the Milky Way. Well, it was like a rollercoaster ride from hell. I couldn't stand it. It just it was too much. It was unbearable, and it only lasted maybe a second or so, and then it was gone.

Then he told me we were going to start transcending or dimension-hopping. He says you won't feel any g-force then, and it went away. It started ding, ding, ding, ding, ding, ding, going through the dimensions, and, like I said, it only took maybe a second or so.

All of a sudden, we come to a stop way out in space somewhere, and I'm looking at the Milky Way galaxy, and you can see it up there. It was awesome, and I loved it. I do almost feel like it was like a reward. That's what it felt like, but these cubicles that they had me in. They told me that we humans, we had to be in them, or he said you know you would die if you weren't inside them. I assume it has something to do with the quick acceleration. People talk about the speed of sound. This was like the speed of thought. It was that quick.

Here is an account that Ron put on his website that has some other details.

On the night of 07/26/2009 I lie down on my couch and immediately see the dull beam of light as before in other previous encounters. Everything turns a dull-looking fuzzy white, and I start to feel g-force that soon becomes very strong. While this is happening, I am face to face with the dark brown entity named Elbe. This same entity told me his name from a previous encounter. When I became awake, I found myself inside a small clear cubical attached to the ceiling of what looked like a large room. There are other cubicles there, along with mine, that have a human person in each one of them. I can see these dark-colored entities moving about below me, and they seem to be busy, but I don't know what it is they're doing. After a short while, an entity stops below my cubical, and then I start to descend to the ground. This cubical opens up at the end, and I step outside of it. I ask him where we are, and he tells me that I'm in one of their ships and that I have to be in this cubical for my protection or that I will die. I can see the other cubicles with other people in them. He tells me that it's time for me to understand what has been happening to me. He tells me that I have been programmed from birth to fly this ship to transport chosen people off this planet to another dimensional Earth in the near future. All communication is done telepathically. After he tells me this, he gets face to face with me as if he is downloading information into me. After a short while, he tells me that I have to be put back into the cubical for my protection again. I walk back inside and sit down. The cubical closes and then rises back up to the ceiling. This cubical looks as if it's been molded into a one-piece unit.

There are no seams anywhere. I'm sitting there watching all the activity below for a few minutes, and then it slowly moves back down to the floor. Elbe meets me again, and he tells me that we are going on a little trip. We both walk over to the center of this large room to a chair and what looks like a virtual control panel that's not attached to anything. Everything in this ship looks as if it's also a one-piece made unit. The floor, walls, and seats all look as if it has been injection molded and is very beautiful to look at. It's all a shiny-looking black plastic or ceramic-looking material with absolutely no seams anywhere that I could see. Elbe has me sit down in this chair, and immediately, I can see through the walls out into space, looking at the Earth. Symbols appear on this panel, and these are the same symbols that I was forced to watch in other previous encounters. There are holes and depressions on the arms of this chair, and Elbe tells me to put my fingers into them and then to lay my arms down into the depressions. What is strange about this is that it fits my arms and fingers perfectly and is very comfortable. Off to my right is another dark brown entity sitting in a chair with a control panel like mine, except that it is in the opposite direction from the one I'm sitting in. This other entity is looking at me, and I can sense that it's a female. Elbe then tells me that when we accelerate, I will feel g-force until we start to traverse the dimensions, and after that, no more g-force will any longer be felt. In a previous encounter, he showed me a device that allows them to travel inner dimensionally. I asked him what am I suppose to do. He told me that it's already inside of me and all I have to do is think about what I want to do, and the ship will respond to my thoughts. I think to myself that I would like to go out into deep space to see the entire Milky Way galaxy from a distance. All of a sudden, the g-force is so bad that I can't stand it, and I feel like passing out. It feels like a roller coaster ride from hell. The stars that I can see outside the ship all turn into streaks of light. This only lasted for maybe a second or so and then stopped. At that point in time, he tells me that we are starting transverse the dimensions. It looks like different pictures flashing by outside one after another and what is odd is that after every hop or picture, there is a different scenario going on outside. This looks like a picture book that you are very quickly flipping through the pages. This all takes place in approximately what seems like 2 seconds or so. After what seems like only a few seconds, we are sitting out in deep space, looking at the Milky Way galaxy. This was so exciting and awesome, something I will never ever forget. Elbe tells me that it's time for us to go back. I think of Earth and where we left from, and acceleration causes the stars to streak, then what seems like a second or so, we are back from where we left, looking at the Earth. He tells me it's time for me to go back home and that he will be contacting me again soon. Everything turns a dull, fuzzy white, and then I pass out and wake up on the couch.

If this story told by Ron is true, it would indicate that he moved probably 50-70,000 lightyears in one second. If that is true, it clearly indicates that we have some problem in our understanding of how time and space work.

I then asked about the craft and if it felt alive to him.

I'm gonna say it kind of sort of felt like it was alive because I could feel it was a part of me. It was almost like an arm or a leg. It's weird. The only way I can describe it is it belongs to me; that's how I felt.

Then Ron mentioned randomly meeting another experiencer who had flown the ship:

> *You know what's weird? I was in one of Barbara Lamb's abduction support groups years ago. There was a man from Casper, Wyoming, there.*
>
> *In talking about his experience, he said they would take him and his young son, and he was having a really tough time dealing with this.*
>
> *He was describing exactly the same things that would happen to me. After the meeting, I was out in the foyer, going back to my hotel room. He stopped me, and he told me he said this flying the ship transporting- he said, 'the same thing has happened to me. I have seen you. I have to let you know. You were in two of my abductions. I have seen you.'*

I asked Ron if he had seen the people he was transporting:

> *Some of them I have. The ones in two cubicles I didn't get a good look at, but in other abductions I've had, they've had me sitting in chairs, big long rows of chairs with people sitting. I've had a man sitting next to me. When we're sitting there, these other people they got their heads slumped down; it's like they're out or not coherent, but this one guy raised his head, and he looked at me. He says, 'man, you have no idea how lucky you are. No idea.'*

I asked Ron if he knew why the people were being transported off the planet:

> *I'm not sure, but I think what's happening is these people are advancing to a stage in their life where they need to advance spiritually. They can't do it on this earth with all the rhetoric, and*

*you know, the wars and stuff, so apparently,
from what I gather from the entities, this other-
dimensional earth is supposed to be a paradise.
No wars, no governments, nothing. It's just
supposed to be kind of like that utopia.*

Kevin J. Briggs

Kevin J Briggs is an author who specializes in consciousness and the connection to ET/UFOs. He is a lifelong UFO experiencer. He recently published a book titled *Spiritual Consciousness: A Personal Journey* which covers 57 years of his experiences of ET contact and UFO connections.

In a recent interview, I brought up the subject of flying the craft and was surprised to learn that Kevin knew both about the consciousness of the craft itself and that he had flown the craft. Here is what he told me in our interview. He related the experience, as many experiencers do, to a condition like an out-of-body experience or on the astral plane. More and more, experiencer accounts seem to point to the fact that a lot of what goes on is not happening in the physical world as we would have believed even ten years ago:

> *I've got one better than that. I'd have to tell you the things leading up to it. There was a time when I was on the astral plane traveling, and I went through the skin (of the UFO), and it was conscious.*
>
> *That conversation,n Alt (one of two spiritual guides who have been with Kevin his whole life and asked him to write his book) said to me, 'Then why don't you travel further, Kevin?' (then just entering a craft)*
>
> *I said, 'well, it's okay for you. You've got a conscious craft here you've got Alt as a companion to travel with. You can go anywhere.'*
>
> *So, he said to me, 'Kevin, why don't you create your own craft?' So, I said, 'well, how would I do that? How would I build a craft - a conscious craft like this?'*
>
> *He said, 'using thought and consciousness.'*
> *I said, 'Okay.'*
>
> *So that evening, I think it was that evening, I thought I'll try this. I'll see if I can create using thought and consciousness. I relaxed. I think about this round craft. I leave my body.*
>
> *I'm in this craft, and I'm looking out through the window, and what I thought were stars were flying past the window, and I thought, 'Wow, I don't know where I'm going. I've no idea. I could get lost.'*
>
> *So, I ceased the experiment, but what I did find out later was that they weren't stars, they were galaxies going past. So, the following day I organized it a little bit better. I thought, 'well, I need to know where I'm going. I need a slightly*

57

bigger craft. I need a bigger window because I want to see it.'

So, I created a larger conscious craft with a larger window and with a seat. I don't know why I need to see it because I'm totally out of the body, and I'll have a look at some star charts during the day. I'll go to Andromeda, and I'll create a mind interface navigation system so where I think is where I go.

So, I've designed it a little bit better now. I've got a larger seat for comfort, although I don't know why I need it. I have a bigger window, and I've got this thought interface navigation system.

So I set off, and I go. I thought I'll go and find them (soul guides). I'll go find out where they are. So I went to Andromeda, and it flew all over the place, and I couldn't find anybody. I did have a thought as I was flying around this planet in this conscious craft.

I thought if I went down into the cloud base and then below the cloud, would people see me as a UFO? I suspect so. I didn't get the answer to that, but I suspect it's just pure conscious energy traveling.

I came back, and I went back into my body, as it were. I stopped the experiment I'm talking about, and then all eight of the council[1] appeared in the bedroom, looking down at me. I said, 'I've just been out looking for you. I've been all over the place in this craft.'

They said, 'Yes, we know. That's why we're here.'

I asked them to explain. They also showed me a large mothership in the bedroom, and I said, 'look - I don't know how can all eight of you be in my bedroom with a mothership at the same

---

[1] The council of eight is a group that Kevin talked about in another part of the interview. He describes and names them all. https://www.youtube.com/watch?v=vuT_3MIR2Yw&t=3312s

time.' They went on to explain about space, time, and dimension, but unfortunately, I didn't understand it.

In relation, you asked whether I have been allowed to fly a craft. They've taken one step further in allowing me to create my unconscious craft. I think what's really happened is they've developed me to the same levels and abilities that Alt and Dee have for our fifth-dimensional beings.

If I could do it - just a regular person, as it were, then we can all have these abilities. We just need to teach them to one another and practice them. That's part of our evolution, I believe, in relation to raising that vibrational consciousness to join the galactic families.

That's what we need to do, and that's where we're heading. It's our natural evolution, but we're being assisted as grandparents teach their children. It's no different. Our uncles and aunts teach their children. I think it's no different from that, really, but we have to be open-minded about it. I speak to many now, and there are many, many working towards this on all different facets, so I think I find it just fascinating and exciting.[11]

Rebecca Hardcastle Wright, Ph.D.

Rebecca is an exoconscious futurist, author, and Coach.

Here is what she wrote about the experience of flying the craft in her book *Exoconsciousness: Your 21st Century Mind*:

Then they escorted me out of the room. I ran up to my favorite place on the craft - the cupola. In the cupola, I was privileged to navigate the craft. I stood at the helm. My mind shifted into a relaxed glide. My small hands one with the craft.

I navigated the craft through space star maps that were stored in my conscious mind. I navigated easily among star systems, and my consciousness fit the craft. We were one.

In 2018, I got to interview Rebecca and ask her about what she wrote as well as why this story about consciousness and UFOs is so important. She started by talking about the importance of consciousness and her work with the late Apollo 14 astronaut Dr. Edgar Mitchell:

Oh, absolutely, and I feel that, especially after working with Edgar and all of them. With all of the international scientists we were working with, there was an urge. There's almost an existential urge going on today in terms of trying to link consciousness and science and consciousness-like technology.

I just have to sit here now after the experiences that I had. I continue to have a lot of just amazing ongoing experiences and see how we are still in the material science so heavily and trying to make artificial brains. You know, put implants in people's brains so that they can do certain things in their bodies. You know, this kind of robotic consciousness.

I just at first, to be honest with you, Grant, first it kind of disturbed me. I'm like, you're going the wrong way, especially after living in DC. I spent probably about three years in DC, just going down that rabbit hole of transhumanism and robotics and artificial intelligence. I met people from DARPA and different, you know, intelligence agencies, and I just continue to be astounded by the information I was bringing forth

To sort of wrap up the information, I was going into DC , I went to yoga. I'd like to go to yoga, and after the class, there was a woman probably in her 50s. She walked out with me to the back parking lot, and we were standing there. I said, 'Oh, you know what are you do here?' Kind of chatting. I was asking the DC question.

I said, 'Oh, what do you do?'

She goes, 'Oh, I work for DARPA. I've been there about 30 years working in consciousness.'

I mean, you could have just knocked me over. I said, 'Oh, that's interesting. That's my field too, and I've been studying transhumanism and artificial intelligence.' I said so, 'Where are you in terms of what you can tell me about what you're doing in terms of artificial intelligence and just the whole linking of consciousness to technology?'

She goes, 'Oh, that's an easy answer.'

I said, 'What's that?'

She goes, 'We're stuck.'

She was so forthcoming, and she said. 'Yeah, we're totally stuck. We're not going anywhere. We're going the wrong way.'

I kinda held on to my yoga mat and thought, and I just looked up at her and said, 'Well do you think maybe it's because you have the wrong definition of consciousness?'

She said, 'That's exactly the problem.'

It's like don't they have any imagination. It's almost like their imagination comes out of Hollywood or something. So I just continue to be stunned. It's like, this is not where our species is supposed to go. Our species is just supposed to be one with materialism.

Actually, part of the work of our Institute is that we're working with psychokinesis in experiments. I mean, humans are supposed to change matter. That's what our job is, and I sat down, and I just wrote a little booklet called on how EXO-conscious humans guide our spacefaring future. How about that for a mouthful? One of the things I do in the front of the booklet is that I look at what extraterrestrial experiencers, or psychic people, really bring to technology, and you know, at some point, scientists have got to look at the fact that if you're an ET experiencer, you're time-traveling. You're bending time. You are moving through space. You're moving through wormholes. You are telepathic. You're doing all of these things that are outside the purview of science that technology wants to get to.

Yet no one ever talks to us. There is such a disconnect. There's like this chasm between experiencers and people in technology, engineers, and scientists, but especially engineers, I would say.

If we're really going to go into space. If we're really going to go into the cosmos in any kind of a meaningful way - like, sure, you know, we can jump up there, and you know to mine the moon, or mine the asteroid. I mean, if we're going into deep space in any meaningful way, it's going to be through consciousness. It's not going to be through these metal crafts, metamaterial crafts, or whatever they are putting together. It has to be a unified field. I guess it's the best word for it; there's a unified field between science, technology, and consciousness.[12]

Suzy Hansen, New Zealand

Suzy Hansen is a lifelong experiencer. She lives in New Zealand and is a former professional educationalist. She is the author of The Dual Soul Connection – the Alien Agenda for Human Advancement:

Well, okay, some years ago, I was actually taken on board a very large grey craft. When I say large, (it was) the size of a town or a city, and within this craft, it was a massive hanger, and there was a variety of crafts.

I was told that I was going to be given the opportunity to go on a flying trip and be able to operate a small scout craft. I was approached by a group of human-looking entities. I'll call them entities because they seemed like superhumans to me. There were much taller than me, very slim, and highly intelligent.

I was taken on board a small scout craft which I was told was one of theirs. Before we took off... I was told that they were going to give me a bit of a surprise, and the surprise seemed to be that after traveling for a relatively short length of time, they opened what I call the window screens on the wall. Looking out, it had gone from darkness in New Zealand being taken on board craft in the middle of the night. They opened up the screens, and I was able to see a hillside covered with vibrant red, orange-yellow, autumn leaves and autumn foliage such as we don't have in New Zealand.

So, from there, I gathered that I was in the northern hemisphere somewhere, like Canada, the US, or maybe Russia. I don't know, but it certainly wasn't the sort of vegetation one would see in New Zealand.

I'd gone to the Northern hemisphere, and it was daylight. I was told that I would be given the opportunity to use two different modes to fly the craft. The first one was with manual, and the other mode, of course, was using the mind to use consciousness to connect with craft.

I was assigned an instructor who was one of the male beings on the craft. So he demonstrated, and he gave me quite a lot of background information about the wobble of the small scout craft that some people often report, sometimes described as a falling leaf movement.

I was told why they used to have to use a manual lever to operate the craft sometimes in our atmosphere according to atmospheric conditions, certain energy points on a craft, the flow of the magnetic field, etc.

First of all, he demonstrated the manual by using this lever that flipped up out of the console in front of me, and I assumed that because I could drive a car, etc., I would find that fairly easy to do. It would be a bit like flying a glider etc., with a little tiny joystick.

However, I soon found that overcompensating on a stick meant that the craft was kind of nearly flipping and moving in a way that wasn't good at all. So that kind of canned the idea that it was going to be easy to do a manual.

Next, I was instructed on how to use the connecting to the consciousness of the craft, which I did by placing my hand on a rubbery panel on the console, and I was given the opportunity to practice this. It was sort of like expressing your intent through consciousness – so, not willingly the craft to go forward, but just by instructing the craft quietly.

It was almost as if your consciousness and the amount of effort, intent, or strength that you put into the consciousness were equivalent to how much the craft moved. That's really the only way I can describe it. The consciousness was so closely linked to the craft there that it was almost like an emotional aspect to it as well. So, you weren't just simply instructing a computer and saying to move the craft forward 15 meters. You were actually moving your consciousness with the whole intelligence and structure and organicness of the craft to move it forward.

I don't think I could adequately put it into words, but that's what I can do. I found this actually much easier than using a manual stick. The instructor said, 'Well, that's because it bypasses all of the brain messages that have to get to muscles and tendons, etc., to make the arm move to make the lever work.'

This is just straight, pure thought and consciousness and connection. So, I was able to practice that for some time, and then they said they were going to take me home and that there would be another surprise.

This one was that we would actually pass through the planet. Now when they said that, I had the most dire feeling of shock, horror, and incineration, but they assured me that it wasn't going to be like that at all. They said that it simply meant that they would move the craft sort of out, or sideways from the dimension, or the status that it was currently in, and they run alongside in this other space, and this other dimension, if you want to put it that way and that when they passed through that space that is taken up by the planet, they would then merge back into this timeline and into this reality. That's the best way I, as a novice, can describe it as a non-scientist.

So, we went through a process where the craft went off beyond our atmosphere or to the very edge of it. I could see the curvature of the earth. I could see everything recede into this beautiful-looking planet with none of the terrible things we know going on the surface, and then we approached the planet at speed, and as that happened on the window screen, on the screen on the internal side of the craft, I could see a vortex or a spinning movement beginning to take place

Then everything went black inside the craft and on the screen. There was just some colored static for a short period of time, and then everything started up again. There was a high-pitched squealing noise that went lower and lower into a deep braking sort of sound. Then the screen came back to life, and everything came back to normal, and on the screen, I could now see that we were in darkness - obviously in the southern hemisphere, as if we had just popped out of a little spot in the sky.

I could see lights along the coastline, which I assumed was the city that I lived in, approaching, so despite the scene and that's where the experience finished, and I was returned home.

After Suzy told her story, I asked her, "What do you think is the role of consciousness? Is it critically important to understand UFOs?" She replied:

I think it's absolutely critical to understand the UFO phenomena not only from the nuts-and-bolts aspects because I am a sighting report investigator. A lot of the time, I get a report sent to me, which when we dive a little deeper, and we interview the people sometimes on video, we get this consciousness aspect coming up within their nuts-and-bolts structure of documenting an actual sighting. It may be that they've communicated with what they think is the craft, or they communicated with an entity outside of it or inside of it.

There's so much that is transmitted to the person through that experience, but also, Grant, I think that consciousness is vital for us to begin to understand if we are in the future to operate the kind of technology that they have. I might also add that strongly in amongst this consciousness is a spiritual aspect because the consciousness, the technology, that involves consciousness that we might unleash on ourselves is totally dependent on the spiritual aspect, or we are going to harm each other seriously, harm other species out there, and wreck on our planet.

We have to have that combined consciousness and spiritual aspect in order to understand, operate, and compassionately utilize this technology.

Donna Lynn, California

Donna Lynn is a lifelong experiencer who wrote the book *From Fear to Love: My Private Journey*. This is how Donna described her journey, which started in 1987 when she saw the alien face on the cover of the book *Communion*. At that point, she knew the events that occurred to her were not dreams:

The book Fear to Love: My Private Journey is basically a collection of 45 years' worth of journals and notes that I've taken from being visited by aliens all my life, from the time I was a little girl. I called them scary dreams and bad dreams and monsters for the longest time.

I was told I had night terrors and that I'd outgrow them, which I never did. It was not until my 20s or 30s that I came to the realization that these weren't just dreams. These were very real. These were real beings and the same ones that kept coming back time after time to interact with me.

They were trying to develop a relationship with me and teach me things, but my fear -my human fear - was so great because they were alien beings. So, by writing it down and reading about other people's experiences (I could come to terms with it).

I finally came to the realization that they were here; they were real. They do care about me, and not just me, but about humanity as a whole. They care about individuals as a whole.

Like so many of the experiencers who have told me their dreams about flying, Lynn described what happened as just part of a larger experience. She dealt with many beings, but the main one that she was in communication with was a 7 foot tall praying mantis being called Croat. He usually had three small greys with him.

Here is Donna's version of flying the craft, which sounds just like all the rest of the stories:

> There have been a few times when I know I've been in a control room, but it's been like a vague memory. There's this one that's very specific.
>
> I remember being taken into a control room. It was a round room. Their rooms seemed to always be round. It was about the size of an average family living room in a regular house, and there were many, many different alien beings.
>
> There were two greys seated at a console right in the center, and they were focused, looking straight ahead where there was a clear window, I guess you'd call it. There were other beings there. Some were scurrying on the floor, and some may be working alongside the wall. I think there were even a couple on the ceiling, all doing work. All were doing their jobs.
>
> But these two greys were the main pilots, I guess you'd say. So when they saw me (this was, you know, later on in years after I'd learned not to be afraid of them and I'd learned to interact with him a little bit), one of them stood up and kind of turned and gestured toward the chair like 'You go ahead and sit here.'
>
> I was a little bit scared, but I sat there at the console and looked and it, and there were hieroglyphs and different lights. The other gray who was sitting next to me, I could tell it was a female. I don't know how but I knew it was a female. Maybe it was the voice because they communicate telepathically.
>
> She kind of lifted her hands up and looked over at me like, 'you drive,' and of course, I was really scared at that point. I was looking out this window, and we were going probably a

thousand miles an hour through trees - literally through the trees. She explained to me, 'our molecular structure was vibrating at a different rate than that of the trees on earth, so we could literally go through them, you know, without bumping into things.'

This is significant because if you look at Suzy Hansen's story, she says the same thing. The being flew the craft right through the mass of the earth's core.

This is also something that has been reported in the AATIP investigation stories. They had reports that UFOs would fly into the water without crashing or causing a wake as they hit the water.

(AATIP Sub-Focus Areas)

The science exists for an enemy of the United States to manipulate both physical and cognitive environments in order to penetrate U.S. facilities, influence decision makers, and compromise national security

- Psychotronic weapons
- Cognitive Human Interface (CHI)
- Penetration of solid surfaces
- Instantaneous sensor disassembly
- Alteration/Manipulation of biological organisms
- Anomalies in the space/time construct
- Unique cognitive human interface experiences

DoD Advantages

- DoD has been involved in similar experiments in the past
- DoD has relationships with renowned subject matter experts
- DoD controls several facilities where activities have been detected

What was considered "phenomena" is now quantum physics

This trait of "penetration of solid surfaces" was evidenced in the famous **SLIDE NINE,** which was used to brief Congress and to play up the UFO threat. The idea was that these possible alien enemies could move through solid objects, and there was nothing we could do about it. They were selling this idea to scare Congress and also probably pointed out that if we could fly objects through solid objects, it would provide us with a technological advantage over all our perceived enemies.

On the other hand, the fact that UFO pilots were reporting that they could fly through physical matter, it raises a big question about UFO crashes. If they can go through things, why are so many crashes?

This is especially true of the 1897 Aurora Texas UFO craft, which crashed and burned after hitting a windmill at 8-10 MPH. Maybe we need to take a closer look at what is really going on?

Donna continued her flying encounter:

> *As soon as she took her hands off, we started to slow down, and I was afraid if we slowed down enough, we'd bump into things. Just as I was thinking that, a building came into view in the distance, a corner that we were aiming right towards. I was saying, 'Do something. Do something. We're gonna crash into that building.' She just kind of looked at me, and we did; we came right up to this building and just tapped it very, very lightly like a balloon would tap against your hand. There was no noise, no injury, and no problems.*
>
> *Then she, a grey alien, actually began to laugh, when that happened, because of my reaction, because I was so scared of what would happen. That was a big turning point for me because it showed me that the grey aliens do have personalities. They do have a sense of humor, and they were kind of teasing me, I think, in a way. I probably could have flown this ship if I*

had taken control and been a little more assertive, but I had the fear, and again they're working on getting rid of fear.

I asked her if she sensed the craft was alive; she said, "Yes, it was like it could sense my thoughts. As soon as I thought it would slow down or crash, there was suddenly a building to crash into."

I've had other experiences. I've been standing outside crafts and looking at it, and it just is like pulsating and humming, almost like an aquarium.

Like, wow, they use plants to filter their air, I believe. They always have a lot of plants around and so like an aquarium with plants in it and fish swimming around and the pulsating and the humming. So yeah, it does seem alive and even conscious, working with the beings that are in it.

Donna also confirmed that she was on board the ship in 1996, where she encountered her 16-year-old daughter, who was being taught to fly the ship, sitting at exactly the same panel that Donna recalled being at. The strange part was that her daughter looked ten years older. The braces were off her teeth, and her hair was longer. She looked over and smiled at her mother.

In 2006, Donna stated that she and her daughter shared a house and that as the daughter was once washing dishes, she looked over at Donna, and it was exactly the same image of her daughter that she had seen ten years earlier.

Captain Joe Vallejo, Former United Airlines

It was just mind and craft.
-Joe Vallejo

Joe Vallejo was a friend of researcher Dr. Joseph Burkes, who works with a worldwide network of activists that he calls

"The Contact Underground." This is where I heard the story. Both men had been involved with Mission Rahma groups in California and had become close friends.

The following is the story that Vallejo told me of what appears to be two separate incidents where he had the dream of flying the craft. Many, including David, a USAF pilot, reported this same idea, David's account is in the following chapter. Here is what Joe told me:

> *The one about flying the craft, you know I tend to forget a lot of these things. I kind of bury them for some reason. I have known Joe (Burkes) for about 40 years, and I trust him. He is a very decent guy, and we have been through different adventures together. We are like brothers. I trust him 100%.*
>
> *When I was a 737 captain, as you know, you go through the progression of different equipment. My first Captain seat was in the 737. I was flying mostly domestic routes and some Central America routes. Then I went to the 757 and 767, and I finished in the 747-400.*
>
> *I remember the second time I was in Seattle on a layover. I called Joe, and I said, 'Hey Joe, I had a dream. This is what happened blah, blah, blah.'*
>
> *Joe said, 'Don't you remember about a year ago you called me, and you said, 'you had a dream that was quite similar like the one you are relating to me now?"*
>
> *I said, 'I don't remember that.'*
>
> *This time around, I said to myself, 'Joe, you are going to remember this,' and I do remember it. I was at the hotel. I spent the night there in Seattle. I had just gotten up. I called Joe. On that second day, I was going somewhere else. I don't remember where I was supposed to go, or to fly to.*

I called Joe, and that is when Joe told me you had a similar dream about a year ago, roughly more or less. I said, 'Oh boy, really?'

Basically, what it was. There was very large – I couldn't see much detail around me, other than there was a gigantic screen. It was almost like a whole wall situation. I was actually standing. I had my hands on something that I could not see. It was like a black flat rounded surface nature. There was another person standing next to me.

I was looking at this gigantic screen, and we were going through some clouds, like coming out of the other side of the clouds. I was the one that was actually controlling this craft. But the situation was that what I was getting, the physical touching was more important. It was some sort of connection or some sort of entrainment. It was like a connection to the brain – to my brain.

It was all or mostly controlled by thought., there was something... Later, they came out with the movie "Firefox" with Clint Eastwood, where there was some kind of mental connection.

Unlike in the movie where he actually has to think, and I think they did that for the benefit of the movie, there was no localization. It was just mind and craft.

Rather than the craft controlling the person, the person controls the craft. It is a sort of augmentation or an extension of the person's brain function. That is all I really remember. I don't know. I have not told anyone else. I have not compared notes with anybody. I don't know how my situation compared with the other guys or anything. This is basically in a nutshell I experienced.[13]

David, a Retired USAF Pilot

Another pilot that told me about flying a UFO was David. He was a member of the Orange County MUFON group in California. He did not attend my lecture but came after the lecture to the restaurant where everyone was meeting.

When he arrived, someone yelled out, "David, you should have been at Grant's lecture. He was talking about flying the craft. Tell him your story."

I asked him if he had flown the craft, and he said yes, but he thought it might be a dream. I said, "Everyone thinks it is a dream. Tell me about it."

Someone spoke up and mentioned David was a pilot, so I asked him what he had flown. He mentioned a number but then revealed that he had flown the F-16. I said, "you flew the F-16?" I was now very excited to hear his story.

He told me he had and that he was a retired USAF Colonel. He had flown in Iraq.

Here is the story he told me. He is moving on to what he thinks is a craft, and there are entities behind him. He does not know if they are human or non-human. He is standing in the middle of the room, and there is a flat console along the one wall.

This idea of feeling that "someone was behind me" is a very common description of a soul guide in a life review. These were described by the 7,000 people regressed by Dr. Michael Newton in his life between life reviews.

The person will describe being in front of a council of beings in a big room setting. The soul guide would stand behind you and to your left.

Other experiencers have been written about with this experience happening to them such as a woman named Mary who Budd Hopkins describes in his book *Missing Time*. In a dream, she is watching a screen on the wall that she is actually able to become a part of the situation that is being shown on it. The whole thing is being directed by someone behind and to the left of her.

David heard someone behind him say, "Go ahead and do it."

David said, "I don't know what to do."

The voice stated, "You know what to do. Just do it."

He walked over to the console and put his hands on the panel. He sensed that he had suddenly interacted with the craft and was surprised that he was instantly flying it. It resembled flying the F-16 fighter jet he had flown. He was able to control the flight easily.

He took one hand off the panel, and he was still able to fly it. Then he took his second hand up off the panel but left it only a couple of inches above, thinking that the craft might stall, and so he immediately put his hand down again.

Nothing happened. David now had both hands off the panel, and he was mentally flying the craft and very amazed at what was happening.

Niara Isley, USAF

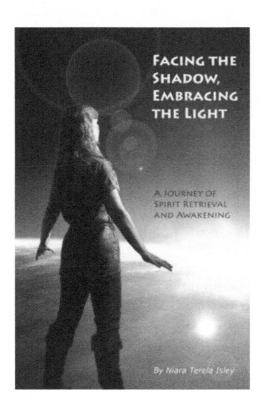

The next story also involves someone in the United States Air Force. Niara Isley. She worked in radar and was stationed at Nellis Air Force base in Nevada:

> *You would sit in this chair in the saucer. It was like a neural interface. You could fly it as easily as moving one of your arms and legs because it slipped right into your neurology.*
>
> *If you want to think, 'I want to go here,' basically, all you have to do is think it. The ship or the computer of the ship was extremely sophisticated beyond anything we had.*
>
> *It would take that desire that you generated in your thought, and it would translate it into something that would create fields in those donut-shaped electromagnetic – I call them donuts, but they basically served the same purposes as an electromagnetic coil.*
>
> *It would generate a field in those coils that would cause it to repel off the surface of the Earth and then move in the direction you wanted it to.*

John Ramirez, Retired CIA

John Ramirez was a high-level analyst at the CIA working on Russian rockets and related electronics. He also had a period where he worked at the Office of the Director of National Intelligence. His 25-year career ran from 1984-to 2009 (GS-15 retired). John recalls that he has been an experiencer from childhood; he was both taken and implanted; he advocates the "need to share," not the "need to know." He believes that one of his roles in life is to talk about his experience and the being he encountered.

In early 2022 he was interviewed by Whitley Strieber, and in the conversation, they got into the concept that the mind is used to fly the craft:

> **Strieber:** *The higher consciousness aspects and the physics are so intertwined. You are not*

going to be able to fly one of these crafts if you are not consciously able to do that. That requires an ability, first of all, to know that you have a second body as well as a first body. There is a soul there too.

You have these levels of being because as soon as you touch what you need to touch in it, you are going to feel that you have become the craft itself. If you don't know what you are doing, you certainly aren't going anywhere

Ramirez: *That's an interesting take, Whitley, anecdotally, and I can't find that source anymore. That source quotes Melchizedek that the government offered him basically a blank check to use the Merkabah techniques to see if he could fly something that they had in their possession because they had no propulsion.*

Strieber: *That is correct.*

Ramirez: *The entire craft would become part of the consciousness of the pilot, so to speak. Without the pilot being able to make that linkage through higher consciousness, the craft is just a hunk of metal.*

Strieber: *It is not quite a hunk of metal because unless you have a clear aim, you even manage to touch it in the right way, you won't be going anywhere. It is becoming part of you, and you are part of it. This business of isolated consciousness inside the body. The U.S. military or the people that are trying to make this work are confused because they think consciousness is isolated. As soon as you actually engage with this thing, your consciousness is no longer bordered by your body. It is in the skin of the craft, which is a very different system. It is not like regular metal at all.*

Then your sense of individuality is changed profoundly. You are someone with objectives and aims that has to do with that craft. Your wishes become your journey, and their journey becomes your wishes. That is the best way of describing that.

Ramirez: *That is a good way of describing it. When I say hunk of metal, I was alluding to...*

Strieber: *It's a hunk of metal without that (consciousness)*

Ramirez: *If the government does have a craft like that in its possession. If other countries have a craft in their possession, it's not doing anything for them. They are trying to make it fly, and they don't know how because there is no ignition switch, so to speak.*

Whitley: *I suggested to Chris Mellon and Hal Puthoff that if they have a craft, they should put it in the Smithsonian. Both of them said that is unlikely to happen. The truth is we are never going to learn how to fly it unless the public has access to it. It is as simple as that. Someone is going to come along. Some 12-year-old version of Melchizedek will walk up to it, and it will turn on, but it will not happen through closed doors... we are going to continue to have this wall between our visitors and us. The wall is secrecy.*

Ramirez: *I don't want to talk too much about the Milab abductions, and this is pure speculation on my part. I am wondering if these events occur because the military wants to have the involuntary cooperation of some of us that have been visited and have had interactions with these higher consciousness beings. They may believe that because we have these higher-level* *contacts, we can fly them and then be taken to some facility with this craft and then coaxed to fly them. I think Melinda Leslie is a good source for that type of discussion.[14]*

In a later interview, Ramirez expanded on this Merkabah idea, indicating that he, too, had traveled the universe like the other sky pilots mentioned in this book:

There was an army study in the Intelligence and Security command which looked at the Robert Monroe Gateway experience, and there was a part in there about vortex fields that when remote viewers go into their deep, deep meditations to remote view that they report feeling a vortex field around them. They are then able to transport their consciousness to another place...

What Tremelo Melchezadek teaches is how to create your Merkabah field around you, and that is like rotating vortices, top and bottom, that will then enable you to ascend your physical body or your consciousness in a sense. In fact, I believe the original Merkabah broken down means light body vehicle, light body ascension, known to the ancient Egyptians.

That has a lot of resonance with me. I felt some of that in deep meditation, and I have said before that people don't need a spaceship out there in the cosmos. I just need me. If I can create something like that in deep meditation. I have actually gone; where I usually go is an ice planet. An icy planet. I don't know why I go there, but that is where I go. That is something I have not really revealed before to any public audience, but I create that field of some semblance to that field. I get this ice planet, and from there, I am presented with information from higher consciousness or what some people call Source. That is where the information comes from.

It is up to me to utilize that information, and I always dedicate these experiences to the good of all. That is how I end that experience, and I thank the cosmos for allowing me to have that experience.

Missouri Experiencer Flies The Craft

This account of flying a craft was told by a friend of ours from Missouri, who had been the Master of Ceremonies at the Ozark Mountain UFO conference for years. In April 2018, we were in beautiful Eureka Springs at this conference where my assistant Desta and I were in a motel room with Linda Moulton Howe and this man, and we were all talking about UFOs.

As the researcher spoke, he started talking about flying a craft as a child. I stopped him and asked if he was aware of my work on people flying the craft. He said, No.

Here is a bit of the story he told us in the hotel room:

Well, you want to go down the rabbit hole? During the last ten minutes, you guys have mentioned three things that apply in all of this. Okay, you'll understand the relevance of this and why I feel I need to tell you all of this stuff to tie into these discussions. It's part of how all this evolves.

When I was 2 or 3 years old -my dad died. I promise I'm not gonna tell you the whole story. Ok, now my dad died when I was 2. Somewhere between the time when I was 2 and 3, I have memories. I have a few memories of being two years old. These are just a few low infant memories.

But I have a very distinct memory of whenever it was between the ages of 2 & 3, and it went on for probably until I was about 9 or 10, I guess - somewhere in there - where as a child, I would have this dream. I would have it when I was little. I had it more often, and it just slowly started going away. Like now I have it - I know I don't think I've had it since I was probably 9 or 10.

When I told him I wanted to put his story in my book, he provided me with a chapter of an unpublished manuscript that he wrote describing the incident. He asked us to use this version of the story:

Wrapped around me was the velvety blackness of space interrupted only by tiny lights like scattered diamond dust - the stars. I am floating in this infinite blackness when, from below me, something comes into view. I sense movement, and it seems I am floating down to see this object. It is sleek and beautiful, disk-shaped, shiny, round, and smooth. A machine made for movement, for flight, it slips fast and silent through space.

I realize that I am moving in unison with this craft, and I sense a purpose to its course, a destination of importance yet unknown. Floating in closer now, I can see a pilot through the metallic exterior of the ship. Suddenly, my perception shifts, and I am inside the ship. I look around and notice that everything is smooth and curved with no sharp edges. The floor bends up at the edge to become the walls that arc overhead to form a dome-shaped room. There are round transparent viewing portholes in the walls and what appears to be a control panel curving partway around the interior. Perched comfortably on a stool that appeared to have been pushed up out of the floor in front of the panel is a man.

I would guess his age to be 45. His white hair is cut short and neat. His features are handsome and distinct but not striking, and he wears an expression of contented wisdom. He is wearing a smooth, satiny white, floor-length robe tied at the waist with a rope belt of a similar make. His sandaled foot to the right is stretched out toward the panel, and the left is folded back under the stool. His left-hand rests in his lap while the other gently covers one of the controls. His gaze never turns from the viewing porthole in front of him. As I am wondering who this man is, my perception shifts again. I AM HIM! It is as if I have stepped into his body like I was putting on the most perfectly fitting suit imaginable.

The body feels comfortable, perfectly healthy, and fit. As my hand rests on the smooth semi-spherical-shaped object on the control panel, I can feel the ship around me as if it is an extension of my body and mind. It responds to my thoughts. It feels so much like a part of me that it seemed as if the ship was made specifically for me, for my mind, perfectly in tune with me. As I look out into the immeasurable expanse of space, I remember everything. I remember that I am a Teacher. My course is set for the small planet ahead in the viewport. The blue planet is known by the locals as Earth. As the white, green, and blue of a world teeming with life looms large outside, an affable feeling fills me - I know this place. I have been here before. I have lived here before in my previous lives, but now I have been called here for a meeting.

My perception shifts again, this time to the end of the meeting. I am seated at a large oval-shaped table in what looks like a large, very modern conference room. There are glowing pyramid-shaped sconces on the walls. I recognize some of the attendees; some are human, some are not human, and some with bodies made only of light. The meeting was long though I cannot remember the details. Now it was time to decide. Because of the seriousness of the matter and the source of the request, the decision was unanimous; we would go to Earth. Our mission: is to accelerate the growth of consciousness in the peoples of Earth so the planet can be healed and peace would reign. Some of us would be stationed on ships, others (with non-physical forms) would work from spiritual realms, and still, others would be incarnate as Earth-born children.

Those born to human families would likely forget their origins until later awakened. Such was my lot. As I stand to leave the meeting, I feel the smooth white robe I am wearing falling to hang at my ankles, calling my attention back to something else smooth and white that triggered this memory in the first place.

The satiny column of milk finishes its dance over the Cheerios cereal that is to be my breakfast, the pouring of which triggered the memory of the cloak I wore in the dream the night before. With a wry smile growing on my face, I turn to my mother and say, "Mooooom, I had that dream again."

"Wha...what dream is that?" she says, a little afraid to ask.

"You know, the one about flying through space and going to that meeting where we decide to fix Earth."

"Ha, ha, oh, that one. Jim was thinking of coming over this weekend. We could take his convertible up to Seven Fingers Lake for a picnic and some fishing," she said.

She hurried about cleaning up the breakfast dishes and tried desperately to change the subject. After all, a five-year-old should not be dreaming, over and over again, about space travel and meetings to save the Earth.

Being a single mother in the sixties was no easy task. My father passed away three years earlier, leaving my mother to raise me alone. Well, not quite alone; my grandmother and grandfather lived with us to help with expenses and babysitting. Having mom and dad around every day to pass judgment on your every move and trying to earn enough money to keep me spoiled rotten was all a woman could take. The last thing she needed was a strange child talking about things she did not understand.

I had been having that dream a couple of times a month for as long as I could remember. It was always the same, and it was always very vivid. As strange as it may sound, it felt more like a memory than the abstract fantasy of a dream. It continued with some regularity until I was ten or eleven years old. I don't recall exactly when I stopped dreaming about the spaceship and the meeting and the mission - it just faded away over time. No matter, I would have other equally strange "dreams" throughout my life.

Denise Stoner, Florida MUFON

Researcher Denise Stoner also told the story of the craft being conscious, even though she did not fly it. She is director of the Florida Research Group affiliation of the UFO Research Center of Pennsylvania (UFORCOP), a Mutual UFO Network (MUFON) National Abduction Research Team member, and a lifelong experiencer who remembers her first experience when she was just two and a half years old. Since then, she has been taken by the same alien at least 50 times:

There was kind of runways that went to the center of this room, but there was an actual liquid that was running under the floor. It was red, but it had a swirling effect to it, and I knew it was very similar to blood, and I knew that it kept this system alive.

I knew that it was running in and out of a center core that I saw, but it had coils that ran around the center core. I also knew that some of the coils had organic and biological stuff within them, and I knew that the central core was more or less a brain of the operation that it could also talk to other systems like itself elsewhere in the Universe, over the huge expanse that they could communicate their location, what they were doing, why they were doing it, and whether or not they would be able to reach each other.

There were so many things that were passed to me in a quick amount of time.

In a 4th November 2011 hypnosis session with Denise, Kathy Marden extracted some intricate descriptions of the craft itself. For example, she would speak of being in a room with its "own atmosphere"... She would elaborate that the room was almost in complete blackness apart from a pole that went from (what is presumed to be) the ceiling to the floor (this detail surfaces in other accounts from people who claim to have been onboard such spacecraft). She would further state that a mechanical device wrapped around the pole, and two arms came out on each side.

Perhaps the most intriguing detail of this strange device in the middle of the room was the notion that "it's alive and the whole thing inside that center block is in motion," adding "it can think...it operates the craft".

Denise additionally stated a strange figure would tell her that this middle pole and device was "capable of shielding itself...of protecting itself...of passing through anything that flying through space can toss at it"... Denise claimed the figure informed her that "this biological machine brought them (the aliens) here in it."[15]

Don Anderson, Utah

Another person who had a clear interaction with the consciousness of the craft, like Denise, was Don Anderson. UFO researcher Preston Dennett researched this case, and Estrella Katarina Castillo was the one who alerted me to it.

Don is an experiencer from Spanish Fork, Utah, who has had lifelong ET experiences, particularly with one grey alien who appeared to have a lifelong friendship that went back to before Don's birth. The grey wore no clothes and never got older.

Like Ron Johnson, the being brought his deceased father in so Don could talk to him. The father had died when Don was three.

Like Chris Bledsoe, Don also described the experience of standing in space with stars all around him. There was no craft or alien being. I know of several experiencers who have reported this. This is almost as weird and off-beat a story as flying the craft.

Skeptics might say that these witnesses are randomly and accidentally all suddenly telling the exact same stories. That belief leads to what Terence McKenna called the limit case for credulity. If someone can believe this happened by accident, what in the world is there that they cannot believe?

What happened next really surprised me. My anger immediately dissipated, and I found myself floating as one on the craft I was on. I held my place with the craft briefly while trying to process what I was feeling. There was no emotion. Only a oneness with the ship. I could feel the ship's consciousness. And the ship feels mine as well.

I knew that it was alive and had a purpose. It had consciousness. It had awareness, and it knew what its' purpose was and what it was designed for.

It could actually communicate with me, and I could communicate with it. I don't think it had a soul, as human beings would associate a soul, but it was alive.

Its purpose was to communicate with the occupants, whomever they were, monitor life functions, and provide for safety. You could link into the ship's mind, if that is what you want to call it, as it was not a computer, and directly communicate with it with your intent alone.

I then understood life is nothing like human perceives it to be. Even those things that appear dead, such as a tree in the forest, even though it is ready to tumble, have life in them. Life is a convoluted thing and varies greatly depending on one's state of existence.

Eventually, after a really quick connection with the ship, I was brought back into my body to a real commotion in the room. The clock on the wall had the hands spinning out of control while the alarm clock on the counter was ringing so hard I thought the clappers would fall off. The paper pad and pencil flew off the shelf, and I could feel the poor grey's thoughts pounding in my head in a frantic effort to gain my attention.

I came to the conclusion that I had probably finished my training for the exercise.[16]

When I talked to Don, I wanted to ask him about his experience with the ship when he was 14 and up in the mountains. He was there in the middle of the night and suddenly found himself on the ship. The only thing he could remember before was being chased down the mountain by skunks. He hid in an outhouse that he found coming down the mountain, and the next thing he knew, he was on the ship. He ended up in a chair:

The chair I was in when they came and got me, I remember that very well. I remember it like it was yesterday.

The arms on this chair had slots where you put your fingers. You put your fingers in the slots, and the foam would just wrap around them. You are stuck there while you are sitting in this chair.

With the arms, you could make the chair move on the way (up or down) or the other way (up and down). If you turn to the left, the ship is going to bank and turn to the left. The same thing happens if you go to the right. It is a holographic 3D kind of thing where you push the arms down, and the ship goes down. It just reacts to you. You are synchronistic with the ship.

I am sitting in this chair which is kind of like an egg. It was like those egg chairs you saw in the 60s, where they had the music blasting at you from the sides. It had foam that compressed into you and was body temperature, so you didn't feel it.

You link with the ship. It is like you are the main computer chip with the ship. The ship had consciousness of its own. It could link to you while you are sitting in this chair. It could monitor to help keep the ship safe and realize with the brain wave where you wanted to go versus where your body motions your body is telling you to do. The brain links with your body much slower and does not anticipate where you want to go in case you panic. Your body may say one thing, and your brain will say something different, like fight or flight... the ship lines up with what you really want.

The chair itself was suspended right in the center of the ship, but it was not connected to anything. It was just suspended in mid-air.

So, you are sitting in this chair with the arm pads and just doing your thing linked up with the ship. It was all a consciousness type of thing.

In front of me, there was a console kind of going around the outside of the ship. The ship itself was silver, and it looked like it had been poured into one mold. There were no welds or anything like that – it was like one piece.

There were two greys at the controls, but it was set very low, like a kid's control panel. It was maybe a foot and a half off the floor. These two greys were there doing their thing. They were doing something with buttons. There were colored buttons. Orange and red seemed to be the main colors. They were just going along, touching these buttons with their fingers, maybe to get the ship to do different things, I don't know.

As they were standing there, the ship gave way, and this screen opened up. It was like HD or more like an LED screen. It opened up, and you could see outside the ship. The clarity was unbelievable. It could see outside, and you could look down and see the tops of the trees. You could see a bunch of grey beings walking around. I don't know what they were doing... that is the ship that (Bob) Lazar described.

The greys were working; the screen opened up, I leaned forward, and boom, we were out and flying through the universe. The trees disappeared, and we were out there in the middle of everything. We are in this place. There are so many stars. The sky is so lit up that I have never seen anything like it. There was light all over the place. There were stars, and there was a huge ship right in the middle of it all. This thing must have been 2 or 3 miles across. It was just huge. It was like a donut. You could hook up to the inside and move right out into these rooms that are on the ship...

I did a consciousness exercise when I was younger. I was sitting in this chair. It was kind of like a dentist's chair leaning back a bit. It was up off the ground. It fits me; it is molded around my body. The kind of stuff they have is weird. It is kind of gel-type stuff. It is molded around you, but it is firm, and it holds you in place... there is a grey behind me who I take to be my teacher. He had been with me before I was born...

This grey guy is sitting to the side of me. He was telling me to focus on this target that was on a vertical column on the ship. They have a bullseye target on the column. He would say, 'See the target, feel the target, be the target.'

He would emphasize that 'Be the target.' I would jump out of my body and jump back in. We were doing this for a really, really long time. I was getting really pissed and upset over the whole thing because I was not making any progress.

Finally, I got really pissed at him, and I said, 'I have had it with this. Screw you. You want me to be the target; I'll be the target.' I just projected myself into the ship, and at that moment, I felt that it was alive. I felt that all the ships they had were alive, but it was not the same kind of life that we would know. It had consciousness, and it could feel me. I could feel it, and I could understand that it was there to provide life support for the being around the ship...

It could feel my emotions. I could not feel any emotions from it... it was pure wonder and amazement that this thing was alive because I really didn't understand the nature of it at the time, even though I had been on that ship before and connected with it.

Don explained one more training he was given that seemed to link to training the mind. He talked about the grey that had always been with him. He had no name, unlike one other alien who did have a name. Don described an exercise type of game that he and the gray played. It sounded a lot like the exercise Pam DuPuis discussed as a small girl, where she and other children sitting in a circle levitated different colored balls and moved them at each other.

He would pass me a plasma ball, and I would move the ball back to him with my mind. We would play these kinds of games all the time.

When I was part of the ship at the time when I got back from that experience, I was actually able to, for a period of two weeks, move a pencil across a table just by concentrating and focusing on it. Gradually that just dissipated... there is a different kind of consciousness when you are on these ships. It is like walking into a room and feeling the change in the room because the environment you are in is really light... you become a part of the experience. You become part of the environment. You walk into a totally different energy.[17]

Peter Whitley, Experiencer from Japan

Peter Whitley is an American who moved to Japan, where he married and now resides. He had three abduction memories, which led him to spend time looking into the UFO mystery.

Peter also had a longtime interest in meditation and took the Monroe Institute's Gateway course. He learned how to go out of his body and found it easy.

With this skill, he used the out-of-body state to interact with the greys. He ran 40 OBE sessions where he went out of the body and could immediately be in a craft interacting with the beings.

Part of what he did was to get to fly the craft. Here is how Peter described the situation, which started with the grey being pulling information out of a wall. It looked like part of the wall as they pulled it out, but then turned into a book (akashic record information?) with information in it:

> *I'll say one more thing about that room that was quite interesting. I went to that room on another occasion, and they pulled another book from the wall. The wall didn't appear to have any books, but they went to the wall, and this white slab came out.*
>
> *Somehow it was communicated to me that the information is actually held within the walls, not necessarily these slabs. As they communicated this idea to me, it became apparent that this ship wasn't simply mechanical. It had some sort of almost what we would say biological or conscious properties as if the ship had a consciousness of some sort.*
>
> *This really shocked me, and so I stopped for a second, and I said, 'So, is this ship alive?'*
>
> *They said, "It's not alive like you consider things to be alive, but the process by which we make this ship is similar to what you would call biology.' I felt that this was very interesting and a bit strange.*
>
> *I did have the opportunity to pilot the ship on one occasion. This was solely what I did. I sat down on what seemed to be a sofa, but I realized soon after that it was more like a molded chair of sorts.*

There was some sort of, I suppose, control panel in front of me. There was a large window or something I could see out of. I doubt it was made of glass. There was this control panel, or what I took to be a control panel. It was out of reach. I couldn't actually touch it.

They said, 'Would you like to try to pilot this thing?' As with most things, they ask me when I'm up there. I said, 'Sure, why not? You know I'm up here at your discretion,' so I said, 'sure, but I can't; I can't reach that console.'

They said, 'You don't need to reach it. Don't worry about that.'

This process happened where I guess my consciousness, and what I earlier referred to, is this ship having some sort of consciousness merged. How that happened, I can't explain. I don't know, but it merged, and I was able to effortlessly pilot this ship.

We flew down. I was physically in my bedroom on the bed during this session. We flew down above the condominium I live in. It's a 21-story, rather large building.

We weren't that high up. We seemed to be about at the level or perhaps even lower than an airplane might fly, and this worried me. I said, 'Someone's going to see us. Isn't someone going to see us, or is something going to happen?'

Again, amused, they said, 'No, no one's going to see us. Don't worry.'

Then we flew back up. I did travel to the moon after that; it was the only other place I could think to travel to. Then the session ended[18]

Wendy Gallant, Canada

Wendy Gallant is a UFO experience from Ontario, Canada, where she's been a sailor on the Great Lakes and the Caribbean for many years. In 2017 she was introduced to

Seeing while Blindfolded and took her first training in Ottawa, Ontario. Wendy became so fascinated that she continued to research and train with people worldwide, including Mihaela Istrati and Mark Komissarov from Infovision, Romania. In this process, she had many experiences, realizing the greater connection with consciousness which can exist and travel outside the body.

In 2020 she underwent self-reflection and a hypnotic regression where she began to uncover her ET experiences. It led to the discovery that she had been allowed to fly the craft.

Here is the story she provided me for my *Paranormal UFO Consciousness* Podcast. Like many of the people who report the flying experience, it took place in what appeared to be an out-of-body or non-local consciousness state. The other thing that matches many of these flying experiences is that someone is often behind the experiencer on the ship, but they do not know who it is.

The third thing is that the being is described as possibly being a guide rather than a separate extraterrestrial. Almost all experiencers have one alien who gives them instruction, guidance, and support. This idea resembles the idea that a guide may be playing the role of an ET, whereas 200 years ago, it might have played the role of an angel.

The last thing Wendy mentions is that she was not sure if it was a real experience. So many experiencers describe their accounts as dream or dream-like. They remember it well but are unsure if it actually happened.

> *I was meditating. It was a really deep one. The next thing I knew, I was over at a girlfriend's place in Romania. I have never been to her apartment before. So I was in her apartment, looking around, and with the time difference, she was in bed.*
>
> *I was looking around, and I noticed the bedding, the pillows, and how she was lying there, and my next thought was, 'Oh my God, I am invading her privacy. I need to get out of here.' So, I left.*
>
> *The next thing that happened was that I was on the ship, and there was a window ahead of me. There was a control panel in front of me. I was looking out. I could see the Earth below me. It was beautiful. The Earth was huge, so it could not have been that far away. A quarter of it showed. It was massive.*
>
> *I was standing there, and I could sense someone behind me. That is all it was, and then I was back in my body.*
>
> *The next morning, I called my friend and said, 'I was at your apartment last night.'*
>
> *She said, 'Oh really?'*
>
> *I said, 'Yah. I want to check some things out. I have never been there.'*
>
> *I asked her what color her pillows were. I said, 'Are they red?'*
>
> *She said, 'Yes.'*
>
> *I asked, 'Is your coverlet paisley?'*
>
> *She said, 'Yes.'*

I said, 'You were on your right side, curled up in pink pajamas?'

She said, 'Yes.'

I said, 'I really was there,' and my girlfriend said, 'I am glad I was alone.'

So, I wondered if I was actually there, was I actually in this ET ship. It kind of made me crazy.

So, I was out sky-watching with some friends, and this one fellow was very psychic. He has all sorts of things happening to him. We were just chatting over this fire, and I was telling him about my experience. He told me to relive it. He said to relive it and make it physical as if you are physically there. Relive it.

I did. I closed my eyes, and I relived it, and when I opened my eyes, I looked, and he had his eyes closed.

He opens his eyes, and he says, 'I can see the being behind you. He's white. He's tall. He's got very large eyes, slanted. He has a tiny nose with two holes. He has tiny, tiny ears and a tiny mouth. The main thing is that he has a ridge going over his head.'

When he told me that, I remember seeing that same vision when Rob (Freeman) took me back to age five. He said that he believed this person was around me all the time, and he got the impression that he was my guide, and he allowed me to see that.

I asked Wendy what happened when she relived it:

I just took myself back, and I was there with my hands on the console, visualizing the Earth, visualizing the console, and visualizing what I was feeling at the same time... I was in awe of the vision of the Earth, feeling someone behind me, and then I was back... I always wondered if it was real... the console was flat, and my hands were just on it. Nothing was said to me.[19]

Gerard Pratt, Retired Army from Britain

In Britain, we have the case of Gerard Pratt, a retired army officer. He, like many experiencers, had some ability to do an out-of-body experience at will. Here is his story of being allowed to pilot the craft in discussion with myself and Sinead Whelehan.

After working a night shift, I wake at 5 pm and enjoy the rest of the day, but as I'm not tired stay up until midnight watching elements of the conference Contact In The Desert 2019 on YouTube.

When my head hits the pillow, I suddenly find myself now standing with a group of mixed-age people, mainly younger than me, probably 15-20 people in number. It's dark, and we're standing in an industrial-looking area in a courtyard area surrounded by warehouses or hangers. An older woman with long-tied, back grey hair approaches us, identifies herself as the leader, and takes charge of the group, asking us to follow her. I think she's wearing a tight-fitting red uniform, like a flight suit of some sort. We walk up a metallic-colored ramp onto a large disc-shaped craft. Once the group is all inside, the door has disappeared, or at least I didn't see it close. I can't remember what was said to the group, but the lady did give us a briefing.

The craft is quite large inside, and the central room we are in is probably 20 meters across and is mainly white/cream in color and very sterile looking. There is no obvious source of light fittings, but it is well-illuminated. I'm almost certain there are other areas to the craft, but I can't be sure and didn't get to view any. A male with dark hair in his late teens walks forward and places his hand on a white panel on the wall; he says a few words, and the craft lifts into the air, probably 50ft or more. I can see it rise out of a round window, the craft spins around, and we land again. Everyone claps, and it's clear he's done well. I place my hand up and ask the lady in charge if I can have a go at flying the craft, and she agrees, pointing me toward the panel on the wall.

I walk over nervously and place my hand on the panel. It feels like plastic. I'm handed a laminated card to read that has a mixture of letters and symbols on it; one of the symbols is a bird. I attempted to read it, but I knew I had got some of the words wrong, and nothing happened. The leader told me to try again and take my time, so I started slowly, beginning with, "I Gerard," It was 15-20 words, and I think it was giving consent or permission for the craft to sync or interface with me. This time I'm successful and suddenly feel a tingling on my hand and feel at one with the craft; the craft appears as if it's alive or maybe artificial intelligence and is able to read my thoughts. I ask it in my mind to rise, and it lifts maybe 20 feet in the night air, so I decided to go higher and then spin the craft around in a full 360-degree spin; I then calmly land it again in the courtyard. I think I would have liked to sip around in it faster, but I get the feeling the craft knew I was a novice. I definitely felt connected, and I could see outside the craft in my mind's eye during this process. I could see all around 360 degrees for absolute miles, and I felt turned in to it all. As I landed, the group congratulated me, and I felt I had achieved something big.

I can't remember leaving the craft or what happened after my flight, but I wake up on a sofa somewhere in a dark room next to where the craft was; I think it's an office connected to a hanger and feeling happy about my craft experience, I sense the presence of the hooded ET being I've been telepathically communicating with for the last couple of months. I now see him standing in the corner, and there is no fear, only joy. I notice 2 of the flight crew, a male and the same female seen earlier, are standing talking in the other corner, so I remain in my sleeping position and telepathically ask for ET being to come closer and not be afraid.

Suddenly, I now feel it standing over me; it places a hand on my head, and I sense a black glove or sort, but I'm sure I see five fingers. I'm now thinking at least it's got a normal hand like us, and I instantly feel a sense of deep relaxation and a feeling of oneness. Also, the being is very proud of my interfacing with the craft and has come to congratulate me. I'm feeling extremely relaxed now and even consider being up early for work, but I'm not bothered. I'm so relaxed and consider having an OBE and slowly begin to drop through the solid soft floor into a room below, observing the molecular structure as I go. It's great; I'm having a full OBE now as I float down into another room below. I'm now more aware and in control and concerned now with the fact that I'm probably about to meet this being face to face as I'm now in the astral plane as I know it. I'm fully aware and free to explore. I'm not scared, just aware as I don't yet know its form. It could be a mantis being, a grey, a reptilian, maybe fully human in form; I really don't know, but this would be a step forward for me, so I need to hold my nerves to do this! I'm well primed and focused, and determined to ask the right questions if I get the opportunity. Suddenly, I was pulled away by the sound of my alarm clock going off, it was 2 am, and I'd got an early train to work to Manchester at 3 am.

Summary: I'm furious with having to get up and break off the experience while so connected, and I feel extremely hazy; this railway job is ruining my spiritual development. On the other hand, I think fatigue plays a part in breaking sleeping routines and enhancing these experiences, and I only had less than 2 hours of sleep, so it's amazing what happened. I'm now driving to work, looking at a beautiful full moon and listening to the song Moving by Kate Bush. I'm weighing it all up, still half asleep, but I feel a sense of oneness with the universe, like my spirit being or higher self is now very present, and I realize how privileged I am to feel this way.

Tress Blair, Scotland

Tress Blair is an experiencer in Scotland who has also been taught to fly the craft. She has one of the highest levels of contact I have ever seen. She also has some of the best photos of crafts, orbs, mists, and beams in the world.

 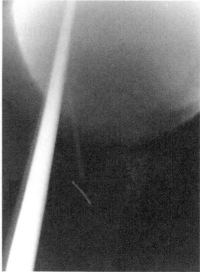

Her description of flying the craft from an interview on her contact experiences is below. I asked her, "You told me they taught you how to fly the ship. Can you describe that in as much detail as you can?"

Well, there's a difference between the children (Tress reports that there are 6,000 on Earth at this time) learning how to fly the ship and somebody coming along and being taken to fly the ship for the first time as an abductee; if you get what I mean.

While we are in class, we are given a symbol. Now, this symbol is what we have through the time that we are learning on the planet. That's our symbol. Mine is like a peace sign.

Now when we have the symbol, and we've advanced to a point where we've learned about why we're here, what we're doing, and that, we are taken into a sort of a room. It's like the functional. It's like everything takes over with all the equipment and all the stuff. We're taken into the room, and we get shown – we are not taken on to the pod as we call it.

We're not taking onto the pod... we are taking in all the pods and the colors and that sort of thing. So once we've taken in all the colors and the pods, it's so difficult to explain to you. When we have taken in colors and the pods in the room, we are shown telepathically how to monitor things, then we are taken into the pod. (The pod is a small craft apart from the main craft)

I've drawn some pictures of them.

So, when we go into the pod, we stand in front of the big pods. There are several of them. They are like rubber, but they are not rubber. They are made of different chemical stuff. There are lights going around the back of them (rubber pods).

We stand, and we have our symbols in our hands, and we have to take on the feeling and the energy of the actual pod. Now the pod is smaller than the actual craft itself, so there are only so many of us in it. We stand and take on the being of the pod. We take it in telepathically so that we are one with the controls and what this pod is.

We do that a few times before we actually get to fly the pod. Once the pod has gotten to know our energy, it's not so much that we know the pod's energy, but it knows our energy. Then we can fly the pod.

We flew the pods, and it was at a very, very fast speed. You would not think it is moving. It is so slow. It is so quiet. It is so peaceful, yet it is flying at such a speed.

It's all mindset. It's like you are connecting to the whole source of the pod through your mindset. It's a structure. You are all oneness. Even if it is different from us, it is all oneness. We are all one at the end of it. It is always in the dark. I have never been in with the light on. It is really black when we go out into it.

You just see the stars. You see the twinkling of the stars, all the different things in the sky as you go flying by. I thought everyone did this. I didn't know.

When asked how many times she had flown the craft, Tress said, "A few."

Tress was asked why they would teach someone to fly the craft, and she said,

They are teaching us all this because they are coming. They are coming down. They are getting ready. The human race has made a mess of the Earth with greed and selfishness, using animals for their own ways, killing, destroying, not having a thought for anything other than what they want... Humans have not been around for very long. It meant that humans were to have loved the Earth, nourished it, looked after Mother Earth, and made it beautiful.

They have just gone all over the place, and what is happening now on the planet? It has all been predicted. They want to save Earth. Earth is very important in the universe. If Earth goes, it is a big structure in the universe that is going to be missing. The whole balance will be out.[20]

Following up with Tress for this book, she told me:

We have been learning about the new transportation; we call them Uma. They are egg-shaped, very dark red in color, and travel at some speed. I was given a lesson on one of them by a species that was like a tiger crossed with a human and was told that this is the future.

Candice Powers, Colorado

Colorado experiencer Candice Powers is a lifelong experiencer who has had many very clear and meaningful UFO encounters. She was a client of the late abduction researcher Budd Hopkins.

She has been interviewed in many videos on my Whitehouseufo YouTube channel, including one on her spectacular triangle UFO sighting. During this sighting, she also witnessed a being with her friend and her son. Both Candice and her son are musicians, and he once produced a song called "Space Overlords," which talks about the triangle sighting that occurred on his 10th birthday with Candice as his witness.

Candice told me her story of flying the craft shortly after Pam DuPuis in 2013. I was floored that a second person was telling this bizarre story that made no sense in our currently perceived 3-D reality.

Candice was not searching for people to tell her flying experience to; she, like many others, saw the experience as a dream. I had to encourage her to do it and asked her to tell it a few times. Another part of the story that many people tell is that they are being instructed to do the flying, but they can't see the beings, humans, or whoever it is directing them. Here is an account she told me about in 2020:

> *It's interesting how there are these connected dreams, so in the vision, which to me I was dreaming, you know.*
>
> *So, in this vision, I thought it was a dream. I woke up, and I guess at some point, I realized that this had happened. I wasn't awake in the dream. It wasn't a lucid dream, and I had never heard this anywhere or from anybody or anything like this at the time. This was quite a while ago.*
>
> *So, I'm on the ship. The ship has a really rounded window that comes around almost to the sides. There's a big, long panel. It's got all kinds of stuff on it, and one of the things that's on it is a half-dome structure.*
>
> *There are these beings on the ship. And I can't see them. I sensed them.*
>
> *I have a sense of these beings, and I don't remember if I was told to do this or if I just did. I kind of think I just did it. If I want to remember, I think I just did it. I just put my hand over the dome. I didn't touch it. I just hovered over the top of it, and I knew that I could tell this ship, you know. I could move the ship. I could fly the ship wherever I wanted it to go by putting my hand over this over this thing. It was like I just thought, 'Oh, I want to go over there,' and then we were there.*
>
> *It was like my consciousness, and the ship were the same. It was like as if the ship itself decided it wanted to go there.*[21]

Jean Kimura

See it in your mind first. Then push the button.
-Jean's instruction on flying the UFO.

This is an important case because it involves two witnesses to the event. It is only one of two in this book where there were multiple witnesses.

The flying of the ship event occurred in 1983 when Jean and two of her friends went to Sedona, Arizona, for a camping trip. They were in Boynton Canyon.

They went to bed at about 11:00 pm. Jean was on the far right, her friend Rita was in the middle, and her friend Pat was on the left.

The next thing Jean knows, she is waking up, and so is Rita. They would learn later; Pat slept through the whole thing and was very upset when they reported what had occurred. She blamed Jean for not taking her. Jean told her she had nothing to do with it and didn't even know how "they got us up there."

The first thought of the two women was that they were standing in a doorway. There was nothing in between. The door opens, and there is St Germaine. Jean was very much into St. Germaine, so this could have been a screen image. During experiencer Yossi Ronen's encounter with entities in his bedroom, he was told, "The way you see us is defined by you... When we visit your world, we temporarily have a physical body defined in a certain way, but it is not the only form, or our original essence, in our dimension; there is no need for a physical body defined in a particular way as in yours."

The being also could have been St. Germaine, as he appears to people. But, whoever he was, he was comforting to the two women.

St. Germain invited them onto the ship. A couple of other people in the craft looked like humans. Nobody looked like an ET or a grey alien.

Jean and her friend were asked to put on garments that were blue one-piece outfits that fit perfectly. The electric fabric bolts run through the fabric. The fabric, according to Jean, looked like it was alive. Then Jean described the flying part of the story:

> *He took us over to the control panel, and the thing I will never forget is we said, 'Yes, commander.' We called him commander because I think in a past life, we worked with him.*
>
> *He explained so many things to us that night. It was incredible. Things about the Earth, the world, the grid system that goes around the country – the electric grid system.*
>
> *We went over to the control panel, and he told us it was up to us what we did. We could go anywhere. We could go and visit different planets. We could go to the past. We could go to the future. Rita and I voted to go to other planets.*
>
> *So, we did that first, and then he asked us what we would like to do next. He said, 'Would you like to drive this?'*

We said, 'Of course. Wow. That's like driving the best car you have ever been in in your life.'

He just showed us what to do. It was very simple. He just told us which buttons to push, but you have to think about what you want to do first. You get to the place you are going to in your mind, and then you are there. You are there in like two seconds.

It's not like you have to travel and travel. It is almost instant. When you tell him what you want to do, you hit the button, and the next thing you know, you are there.

The panel was very nice. It was silver with colored buttons. The whole place was big inside. It was large and very spacious.

It was very clean. Everything was neat and tidy. It looked very sophisticated, and this was 1983.

He was so kind and so polite. He just treated us to this incredible experience. It was amazing.

They took us back to the tent and let us go back in, and they closed the tent. When they were closing the zipper, that is when Pat woke up. She started screaming at us, saying, 'Why did you leave me here all by myself all night long?'

She never talked to me again after that because she blamed me. I kept telling her, 'We did not do this on purpose. We woke up, and we were there already.'

When I opened my eyes, the craft was still up above us. It was right over the tent. There was this six-foot window in the tent. I said to Rita, 'Oh my God, there's the ship!' So we watched it, and as we watched, they left.

We were gone for hours, which made Pat so mad.

When they returned, they were on the same page about what had occurred. "I would start a sentence," said Jean, and Rita would finish it.

I asked whether she felt the craft she flew, and she said:

> *I felt that we did because it was so instant. I still can't understand how we could instantly be somewhere. That was the most amazing part. It was very instant. Everything was instant and so easy. It wasn't hard. Everything was very grateful and easy.*

Suzanne Chanceller

Suzanne is a lifelong UFO experiencer. After reading Whitley Strieber's book *Communion* in 1987, she began to uncover memories of visitations from entities that she felt began in 1966 at her childhood home in Pasadena, California.

She kept her experiences private for many years but eventually started to blog and hosted a podcast called *Random Alien Brain Droppings*. This was also the title of her blog, where she interviews other experiencers, authors, and researchers on the subject of UFOs, abductions, and all other high strangeness occurrences that seem to surround the phenomenon.

Suzanne was of interest to me because of her story about the beings flying the ship below, but also because she is one of two witnesses I know who were shown a giant 3-D holographic equation on board the ship so big you could walk around in it. Like the other witness to the equation, Suzanne received the hint that they might have the cure for cancer.

Here is her description of the being apparently operating the ship:

> *They were all doing something. It was like they all had a job to do. They were like little busy ants just working away at controls that you couldn't even see; I wish I could explain that better. It was almost like there was a cylindrical*

counter enveloping the room, and as they waved their hands over the counter, it was almost like they were adjusting things and settings, or that is how they maneuvered the craft. I am not sure.

Now another thing about that is there were two humanoid-type beings doing the same thing. They were dressed in uniforms. There was a boy and a girl, and I would say they were about in their teens. They were the only two that turned around and made eye contact with me. They seemed very uninterested in my presence there.

Paul Hamden and the Zeta Race

Paul is both a medium and lifelong contactee who has developed a strong, evidence-based relationship with the Zeta race. Their contact began at a very early age for Paul, continuing into his adulthood, and today, they still have regular contact.

In the late 1970s, the Zetas' brought a 'tic tac' craft within ten meters of his residence, and he and his three friends were able to see two beings on a craft during the encounter. Ten years ago, Paul organized for a craft to come to a large property; there were about 20 people present who attended the craft landing; the beings came out of the craft and then walked around them for under one minute.

Paul facilitated energy-related interactions with the Zetas, and there have been many books written, such as *A Primer of the Zeta Race* and *The Zeta Interviews*. Paul's latest book called *The Zeta Mind,* is a short handbook written for individuals who wish to learn how to safely contact their point of origin race.

In an interview with him, he indicated that the craft was conscious and that the craft was piloting itself. I asked him if all crafts were conscious. He said, "No." He then explained:

The
ZETA
Mind

CONTACT

Paul Hamden

This is the difference. With the Zetas and what is not known about a lot of the Zeta technology is that they are actually using cellular genetic matter to create the craft. And one of the current technologies that they are using is to use female eggs to create small crafts. When I say small, I mean just a couple of meters across. What are the capabilities of their technology to blend with eggs so that they can produce crafts that way?

To me, they are looking at what is taking place 500 years from now. If they disclose their presence to us, they are going to want to share their technologies with us. In doing so, we are going to want to create a craft and travel.

In doing so, we will have to use our genetic makeup to create our own craft because we will not be able to interact with their craft because we do not have the level of consciousness to do so.

So, if we can create our own craft that understands our consciousness, then we will be able to pilot our crafts ourselves.

Then I mentioned that I was working on a book on people who pilot crafts; Paul had a different take on people claiming to fly crafts:

Personally, I first have to state that the number of people who believe they have been allowed to fly the craft is just a screen memory that they are given. It would be like saying to a child, sit on my lap, you can hold the steering wheel, but I will actually be driving as you put their hands on the wheel...

Probably 30, 40, or 50 years ago, that is how you did teach someone to drive, sit down and drive around.

When you are on a craft, it may look like you are piloting the craft or that you are actually in control. But think about it. You have a craft that moves that fast and has the ability to slam into the planet's surface. They are not necessarily going to give you control over this craft when their lives are at stake, but they do realize that humans like to put their hands on it.

So that is one way. There is training that you can be given in regards to working with craft, but you won't be allowed to connect with the craft initially with consciousness because you don't have the capacity to do that. There are always wonderful stories of people connecting with crafts.

When I was on the craft, I was on crafts with Syann as well. It was very interesting. They were trying to teach me how to move the craft forwards, backward, and sideways. I had to use manual controls. I was not allowed to interface with the craft at all, and to be honest, that I didn't crash this thing was a miracle.

I couldn't, even after half an hour. Their technology is different, so if you are on the console, you slide your fingers down, up, and sideways. The problem is that you are no longer in a three-dimensional cognitive space. You are in a multi-dimensional reality.

Inside the craft, while you are trying to do this, you are in a heightened level of frequency, so to try and do just these three actions requires a lot of concentration, and your mind keeps forgetting what you are supposed to be doing.

So to tell me that I am now going to be piloting a craft and embedding my consciousness with that craft, I just don't see how that would even be possible, even with training.

I then asked Paul about crashes and crafts that are reported to go into the water at high speeds that don't seem to be affected. Paul replied.

Crafts are designed to be operated at designed frequencies. So when they are flying at the Schumann's frequency, the craft, and I know this is difficult to understand, the craft actually becomes unstable, and the slower they are meant to go unless they are actually descending. If they are descending, it is not a problem; they know there is a trajectory that they are going to be working on, but if they are going to move and navigate at speed, it is very, very difficult. That is why crafts do crash at slower speeds. They are not designed to do that.

The crafts are conscious beings, and they are able to navigate outside the earth

I then asked if he maintained that people were being shown screen images and not flying the craft, how could he be sure he did not see a screen image. He answered:

> *Because we asked to be allowed to bring a drone in-a small drone craft that had no physical containers on it, just as humans have drones, they have drones as well. They are not populated by anybody. We brought a drone in and hovered it above the house. We took a picture of it. It was at night. It is super difficult to see, unfortunately. It was like a triangular drone craft. Syann saw it as well... that is why I was shown how to do some simple rudimentary controls but to do it consciously.*

Desta Barnabe, Canada

This late addition to the book shows that men don't listen well. I had completely forgotten that my assistant Desta had detailed to the Winnipeg UFO Meetup group and me years ago a story about how a sparkling, grey-like being explained to her how to fly the ship.

This story begins with the idea of *Contact Modalities*, the book I wrote with Desta, where people can access material outside their normal conscious conditioned mind of memories and feelings. Desta's story is also linked to an account told by Stanford scientist Garry Nolan who has worked with Dr. Kit Green on studies with UFO experiencers and how their brains may differ from the general public.

Garry talked about a message he received in the middle of the night. "This is how you make contact." He said he was "fully awake" when it happened:

> *I once had an experience in London that I don't understand to this day. I don't know why this always happens at 3 a.m.... I woke up, and my whole body was pulsing with some sort of electric fire – like nothing I had ever felt before. I could hear it and feel it, from the tip of my toes to my fingers – my whole body. Right as I woke up, it wasn't really words, but it was clear. The words were, "this is how you connect." It went on for about 15 seconds, and I said, 'whatever this is, stop. This has got to stop,' and it stopped.*
>
> *So, I was clearly awake. I had control over it but again, where did this voice come from. Maybe it was a dream. The voice was of a dream voice of some source, but the feeling was not. I had never had any feeling like that before.*
>
> *Interestingly, the next evening it happened again at about the same time, but it was only a fractional sense of it.*[22]

In an interview with the Winnipeg UFO Group, Desta described how she was shown what it felt like to be in a theta trance-like state by a sparkling being who appeared behind her. In our book *Contact Modalities*, we write about this state of mind and how this applies to flying the flying saucer; what she revealed matches exactly what the three dozen other witnesses have said. Desta was talking about trying to attain this specific mental state where she could force herself to get out of her body and astral travel. Like the experience of Don Anderson, she was also told that to fly the ship, you needed to BE the ship; this is integral in flying it. Another similarity in Desta's story is that there is a being behind her who touches her shoulder during the experience. To set the stage, Desta was practicing how to have an out-of-body experience and couldn't get into the state of mind she called the Theta state. She tried and tried, and then one day, in frustration, cried out to the universe to help her:

'How do you do it? I can't get out of my body. I can't talk to my higher self. So, like, what's the trick here?'

And so, this being - this sparkling thing, I don't even know if it was a being. It was very strange like the body shape was maybe similar to a grey (alien), but it wasn't grey. It wasn't, you know, grey, and it was sparkling.

So, I guess it wasn't a typical grey alien figure. I don't know what it was, but the thing came to me and said, 'Oh, you want to know what it feels like to be in theta? This is what it feels like to be in theta,' and it touched my left shoulder with its right hand.

It touched my left shoulder; that's why I knew it had a really bony, long hand or whatever; it touched my shoulder.

*It said, 'Oh, you want to know how to get into theta? This is how you **get** in theta.'*

I had the like experience where it was inside my brain or something. I felt my brain turning down, and I saw a knob like a stereo, you know, from the 90s or whatever, like with a big giant volume knob. So I saw the knob turning down, and I felt my brain waves, I guess, in my head turning DOWN.

It just felt like; I don't know how to explain it- like it was turning the knob down, turning my brain signals down. It was similar to one of the ways that we regress people. You imagine yourself walking slowly down a flight of stairs, and so I had the feeling of DOWN, DOWN, DOWN as my brain was being pressed down. I was seeing the big knob turned down, so it was just like DOWN in three different kinds of ways.

*The being kept turning it down, and so I felt my thinking also turning down. I could feel, and that's what it was - this being was trying to explain to me that THIS is how it feels to be like in theta, how it **actually** feels. So I had the feeling the entire time of DOWN until the very end of it. I felt like I had just walked down, you know, a million stairs.*

*Then I was standing in the middle of the earth or something, and it was like a giant parking lot. It looked like a parking lot, but I was in the middle of the earth. As I finished descending the stairs, my brain was basically shut off completely. It was so absolutely non-existent of anything. There was like, it was like, **nothing**. I was in the middle of the earth by myself in a completely, I don't know, like an isolation tank. It was like, no anything. No little bit of noise. No feeling. No emotion, no anything. It was complete isolation, and it shut down my entire brain.*

So, they're (the sparkling being is) saying this is how it feels when you get into theta, and then because I could now feel how it felt, I felt what it was like at the end. In the end, it was unlike my normal meditation, which never felt like that. It was not like that at all. I was pretty good at meditating. I could meditate for hours and hours and have not one thought, but nothing felt like how this thing felt, and when they did that, it was like, 'Okay, like, I get it!!'

I was telling you (interviewer Mark Olsen) yesterday they had an analogy they were trying to make. Now, this may be why the "Contact Modalities" (book) was so interesting to me as well. So first, they said one thing (which I've never remembered - even in my original notes that I wrote right after this happened, I have a big question mark).

They were trying to make it analogous to something, which I don't remember, so they said this is (being in theta) the same thing as this (which I don't remember). Then they said, this is also the same thing as flying the ship.

Suddenly, I was then at the front of what I thought was or what they were trying to make me think was a ship. They said, 'It's the same thing as how you fly the ship.'

I didn't fly the ship like many of Grant's interviews with all these people who flew the ship. But they flew the ship with my brain for me, and they let me feel what it felt like to do it.

They were saying, 'This is also how you connect to the ship,' and so again, they used my brain to show me how the brain connects to the ship. It was exactly the same thing where it's the knob turning down the pressure. Like stopping all the stuff in your brain and walking into the center of the earth, which basically means you can connect with the ship. So the way to fly the ship is the same as astral travel, which is the same as connecting to your higher self: you have to get into a state where you feel absolutely nothing. Then, you just have to think about the ship, and you can fly it wherever you want. Then they said the final thing, which was also the same as travelling through space.

So, as I was on the ship, they basically said like, 'Where do you want to go?' and (I saw out the window) just a zillion stars. So, I just randomly pointed to one star. Then they took my brain, and they made it; they showed me from where we were, to, in a split second, to be at that star or the place I pointed to. They used my brain to bring us there.

So, anyways they were just trying to say this stuff is all the same. It doesn't matter if you want to fly the ship, command the ship, be a channel, or astral travel, or all this stuff; it is all about getting to theta. BEING in this theta state of mind. They never said the actual word theta, and I don't even say that anymore because I don't even know if it is theta. It's just getting into that state, which is exactly (what we wrote about in) the Contact Modalities book. It's just about getting to the trance-like state. So, It doesn't matter what you do. You can fly the ship. You can control the ship. You can travel through space. You can do all this stuff. It's all the same thing. What matters is how and where your brain is – mentally or psychologically, or psychically.

It is happening inside your brain, and that is how you get to do anything. That is what they were saying - from what kind of things you're doing, like trying to get out of your body (astral traveling) to flying a ship across the universe. It's the same thing; we use the same thing (it's a state of mind, the contact modality of a set brain wave state)...[23]

Enrique Villanueva, Peru/California

Enrique Villanueva was once a member of the Latin American group called Mission Rahma. They use a Merkabah meditation as a part of their group gatherings. Villanueva is a contactee from Peru who annually leads a contact meditation group at Mount Shasta.

Villanueva talked about encountering another group in Los Angeles, where he lives, that was making some bizarre contacts which Villanueva found troubling to understand. Yet as a part of this encounter, Villanueva had an experience of merging with a craft. This is the same experience that many other people describe in this book. However, he had never publicly discussed this part of it until I contacted him about the Merkabah as a means of moving around inside of this other reality. In a part of the conversation, Enrique told me the following story:

I had an experience where I went inside a spaceship from a civilization supposedly from the future earth. The ship was semi-inorganic and organic, was intelligent by itself (a form of AI), and I fused myself with its core, so it became an extension of myself. The story is long and too crazy, so through the years, I had avoided talking about it and taught the people only the good side of the contact leaving the aspect I cannot comprehend for a more personal inquiry.

The Portal Xendra Connection

The focus of what he and the other people he was working for seemed to want to obtain and develop was how this technology enters this reality and leaves as easily as it entered.
-Jim Penniston describes what he was told about a government program looking at UFO experiencers.

My wife does have a time machine of sorts.
-Dr. Ron Pandolfi, former head of the Weird Desk at CIA.

Jim Penniston is one of the main witnesses in the Rendlesham Forest Incident when in 1980, a craft landed outside a USAF base in the UK. A few years back, Penniston met with Dr. Kit Green in Rockford, Illinois, along with his lawyer, Pat Frascogna. Green was the CIA control officer for the SRI remote viewing program in the 1970s. He was also the head of the rumored "weird desk" at the CIA, where UFOs and other paranormal phenomena ended up.

Penniston was determined to know what exactly Green was up to by asking for both Penniston's DNA sample and an MRI of his brain. During the two-day meeting, Green told Penniston that he had contacted him because he was working "with a group who are exploring cases that need to be looked at."

Penniston pressed, saying, "Are you doing subcontracting work for the government then?"

Green replied, "Yes," and said he worked for Bigelow Aerospace "with a group of eight other scientists and medical professionals."

Green claimed the program had to do with the propulsion, to which Penniston replied, "Oh, come on. It is not about propulsion."

Green replied that propulsion might not be the right word. But, then, he clarified his statement to Penniston, saying:

> *Ok, so the real meaning of my point of view is that this is not just about Rendlesham Forest itself but also aspects of the phenomenon we have seen in other witnesses. And rather than propulsion, we want to understand exactly how the technology enables dimensional travel, so in a sense, it is propulsion.[24]*

Penniston summarized his understanding of this: What Green described sounded like portal technology. Penniston said:

> *The focus of what he and the other people he was working for seemed to want to obtain and develop was how this technology enters this reality and leaves as easily as it entered. The phenomenon seems to involve inter-dimensional travel, and understanding this could be the 'Key' to three-dimensional space and time.[25]*

The work Green was doing for the government under the Bigelow contract involved experiencers. That work also seemed to be centered on the portal idea of popping in and popping out of our 3D reality.

This would tie into an audiotape that leaked a few years back. It appeared to have Kit Green interviewing an intuitive woman, looking for answers about the intelligence behind the phenomenon. Later, I was told that the intuitive, who we shall call CRM, who Green described on the audio[26] as being 95% accurate in her assertions. This would make her the top psychic being used in the Defense Department's investigation into experiencers who have had close encounters with UFOs.

*There is a 4ᵗʰ dimensional portal in this
area, in the area of the (cardinals?). It's very near
the site. The portal, which is a portal of 12
dimensions, is related to an underwater base
near the Catalina Islands off the coast of
southern California (almost the same location as
the Nimitz carrier group UFO encounter in
2004). At that date and time, a craft landed, and
occupants appeared in this dimension.*

*At this point, Green stopped her saying,
'Halt, halt. I want to make sure to write down the
base. You are saying Catalina Islands?'*

*CRM continued by describing the beings as
partly extraterrestrial and some human...this is
part of our ongoing education.*

The Mission Rahma group, where Villanueva spent
some time training, also points out another form of transport
between one place in the universe and another. Like the
people moving from one place to another inside the ship,
Mission Rahma protocols also describe this as instantaneous.

The method they describe is unique to the group. They
call it a Xendra, and they are formed when a being from
another planet wants to interact with us humans here on
Earth.

Sixto Paz Wells, one of the two original founders of the
Mission Rahma group in Peru, described the first of his many
Xendra incidents in 1974 when he and his brother first made
contact with the intelligence through automatic writing.
"Through the passage, a person who enters a Xendra is
essentially dematerialized."

*Oxalc (the being) had informed Sixto that
this door of light was called a Xendra or
interdimensional entrance. They used it not only
for projections such as the one we had just seen
but chiefly as a means of transport which
allowed their displacement from one place to
another in only a few seconds. The spaceships
also used this interesting device to jump great*

distances in space and avoid the inconvenience of the relative action of time during and at the end of their journey. According to the extraterrestrials, there are four types of gates or Xendras. Number four is normally used for physical transport. [27]

Another Rahma-trained individual, Ricardo González, talked about his many encounters with the Xendra phenomenon. In his book, González described Xendras as:

... an artificial concentration of energy that allows dimensional experiences at different levels. These portals, according to what the extraterrestrials have told me, are not entirely physical. They function more as holographic environments where a person can be projected from one place to another or receive information packets complete with guidelines and instructions for the short time they are in that energy. [28]

Antarel is one of the key UFO entities who has engaged with the Mission Rahma people. This is how he described the Xendra to Ricardo González:

We know that you have been reflecting on it: there are different doors, folds, and experiences, and all of them occur at different levels according to what we schedule and also in line with your preparation. But even in the case of some dimensional doors that can be used to physically transport either you or us if we pass through them, the energy in motion is more subtle and connects with other types of forces. In other words, it is a parallel, holographic reality. Because of it, in the midst of these experiences, you appear luminous, and you perceive things differently even if you are 'physically' there.

The Xendras were established from a contact perspective as the main tool for close encounters with you. It is a less traumatic way for you to have a meeting with us and, at the same time, gives us the means to teach you about other inter-dimensional realities that will have a foothold on Earth in the near future. The physical contacts which involve a closer relationship with us are individual. On a few occasions, we attempted encounters with groups but found them largely unsuccessful.[29]

Government intelligence officer Ron Pandolfi also promoted this portal idea. Pandolfi and his wife Aliyah have provided material to a man named Dan Smith, who has put out the information on his internet blog. Aliyah and Smith were also hosting GoToMeetings online from time to time, where the concept of portals was discussed. They have even hinted that technology exists to produce portals.

The portals they are referring to may be related to the Xendra mentioned by Mission Rahma and the instant propulsion described by people who have flown the craft.

Pandolfi spoke, on one occasion, about what seemed to be a portal or Xendra while he was on a cruise through the Panama Canal. Sitting beside his friend John and referencing a place in the desert where there is a portal, this is what he said:

For thousands of years, people have speculated about what it is like to enter the entrance to another world. Now we are on the cusp of a breakthrough where the door is about to open. In John's next adventure to the desert, he will be joined by a couple of people sitting here, which will bring them through the doorway and into the next world and then back.

From all these stories, we see that there may be a propulsion system that instantly moves people and crafts from one point in the universe to another instantaneously or to an alternate reality where the UFO intelligence resides.

It also shows that our ideas of time and space may be way off the mark. It supports an idealist view of reality where consciousness is primary, everything is made out of consciousness, and what we think is the primary determinant of what happens, where we go, and how we get there.

In another instance suggesting consciousness may be the key, I was lucky many years back to meet the elusive Tyler D., who famously appears in Diana Pasulka's book, *American Cosmic*. Tyler D. is said to be the main UFO expert at NASA. He showed me photos of the painting taken inside the old Hughes Aircraft building outside of LAX in Los Angeles.

In one photo of a painting, two men were flying through space. After showing me the images, Tyler told me the building was where the rumored CIA's *jump room to Mars* was and that this painting of the two men was right outside the elevator. That was the key to the story: people were being teleported to the red planet from here.

The jump room to Mars always seemed like a crazy story, but I had to rethink the whole thing after Tyler showed me his photos. I was left wondering if the story was so crazy; why was Tyler there photographing the lobby of the building where the jump room story had supposedly taken place?

Whether the government has a portal or not is hard to determine. However, there was a lot of effort put into this story by Pandolfi to get people to think this might be the case.

Near the end of the search for this government portal, I concluded that it was a waste of time as I would never find out. In a last-ditch effort, I reached out to a close associate of Pandolfi's and said I was looking to pack it in. I asked him, "Based on what you have heard, should I go do something else instead of hanging around?" He thought about it and said, "You might want to hang on." A couple of years later, I am still waiting.

The Modern Musicians

The Moody Blues

"The Lost Chord" is a song composed by Arthur Sullivan in 1877 after receiving it in a dream while sitting with his dying brother. After waking, Arthur could only remember part of the melody he heard in the dream - thus the song's title, "The Lost Chord."

Sullivan was one of the most famous composers of the day in Britain, penning songs like *Onward Christian Soldiers.*

This song was the first song ever to be recorded on the phonograph by Thomas Edison in the 1880s. Although not written for sale, the song became the biggest commercial success of any British or American song of the 1870s and 1880s.

Two weeks after the sinking of the Titanic, "The Lost Chord" was sung by Enrico Caruso at a benefit concert on the evening of 29th April 1912 at the MET to raise money for the victim's families.

Years later, the rock band The Moody Blues would do an entire album on the theme of the Lost Chord. Mike Pinder wrote part of that album, and the Moody Blues recorded the song *The Best Way to Travel.*

The song clearly points to what we have discussed in this book and what experiencers talk about when flying the ship. That it is done with the mind, almost like an entangled particle on the other side of the galaxy changing its spin instantly when the spin of its entangled partner is changed. Here are the lyrics to the song:

And you can fly
High as a kite if you want to
Faster than light if you want to
Speeding through the universe
Thinking is the best way to travel
It's all a dream
Light passing by on the screen
And there's you and I on the beam
Speeding through the universe
Thinking is the best way to travel
We ride the waves
Distance is gone; will we find out?
How life began? Will we find out?
Speeding through the universe
Thinking is the best way to travel
And you can fly
High as a kite if you want to
Faster than light if you want to
Speeding through the universe
Thinking is the best way to travel

The song and its lyrics start to make sense when it is revealed that the song's writer and the rest of the Moody Blues were abducted from the motorway coming into London, England, from a show they were doing in Manchester.

Band members Denny Laine, Mike Pinder, Ray Thomas, and Clint Warwick were on-board. Pinder was in the back seat and was the first to notice the red light of the UFO. He encouraged the driver to stop, and the whole band watched it land on the other side of the motorway. It was drummer Graeme Edge who seemed to have become most transformed by the sighting. As in many encounter-type sightings, all the cars on the road seemed to disappear. Graeme stated in one interview:

At first, I was convinced it was an aircraft...
however, it acted most peculiarly. What was
really strange was that when this thing passed
nearby, there was no traffic on the road in either

direction, and there were none of the usual nocturnal animal or bird noises.

Mike Pinder described the sighting and the three hours of missing time that the band experienced this way:

> *In 1966... with the first band, we were coming back from Manchester around midnight, and we always wanted to get back to London before dawn; otherwise, we'd have trouble getting to sleep. We were coming down from Manchester on the day they opened the M6 motorway. So, we're driving home at about one o'clock in the morning, and I'm sitting in the back, and I'd put my head back and look out the back window and look at the stars. So, we're driving and probably doing sixty miles an hour. There was this red light, and I said, 'I don't remember that radio station around here.' So, I told the guys to pull over, and we got out. We all looked over the top of the car, and there was this red ball kind of thing moving across the freeway that turned into a square ... like a red dice. As it approached us, it got bigger and bigger, and we were all sort of bathed in this blue light. We ended up getting home three hours late and wondering what the heck was that? ... So that really solidified my nickname of 'Micky the Moonboy' as a kid. I was always interested in the moon. ... Read Zecharia Sitchin ... he's the guy!*

The Moody Blues wrote many songs with in-depth lyrics, and many researchers confess that they feel driven to listen to their music.

The Moody Blues have a lot of UFO-related stories that they don't reveal publically. In a conversation with a crop circle researcher, Pinder stated that he and his lead guitarist remember being told about their job in this life as musicians before they were born. Their job would be to raise the consciousness of humanity with their music.

Talking about flying through the universe by just using your mind in 1968 was unheard of. It leads to the possibility that, indirectly, the song was spelling out how the saucers really move throughout the universe.

Cat Stevens

Cat Stevens (now Yusuf Islam) grew up in London, England, under the name Cat Stevens. Yusuf sold 40 million albums in just the 1960s and 1970s.

In London, he used to sit on the roof of the complex where he lived and look at the sky. This interest may have stemmed from the fact that aliens once abducted him. He told of this encounter in the 1970s:

> *One night I was lying back in bed, and I saw this flying saucer shoot across the sky and stop over me. And it sucked me up into it. When it put me down, I shot up in bed. I knew it wasn't a dream. It didn't feel like a dream. It was real; I know it was real....*

Stevens wrote two songs about his experience. One was "Longer Boats," in which he stated:

> *Longer boats are coming to win us*
> *They're coming to win us; they're coming to win us*
> *Longer boats are coming to win us*
> *Hold on to the shore; they'll be taking the key*
> *from the door...*
> *Raise your mind up and look around*
> *You can see them; yes, they're looking down*
> *From a lonely asteroid in a vacant void.*
> *Dyin', but not destroyed.*
> *And "Longer Boats."*[30]

Then there are the lyrics for his other UFO song, which refers to being on the ship. The song was called "Freezing Steel." Stevens makes many references to indicate he is talking about being on a ship, including the fact that the ship had no guiding wheel. Experiencers often describe this type of navigation:

I've flown the house of freezing, the house of freezing steel
And though my body's back, I know it can't be real
'Cause I've been on that house without a guiding wheel
The house of freezing steel...

Up on the house of freezing, the house of freezing steel.
I made my mind up then to get me to the wheel
I made the cabin door; the pilot turned around
He said we're Venus bound
Oh, please take me home
After all, I'm only human, and the Earth is where I belong
I must have looked pitiful to this freak without a face
'Cause as he touched my head, I saw myself back in bed

These lyrics are significant because they reference the fact that there is no guiding wheel. Witnesses in this book are saying that this is because the mind is the thing that guides the craft.

I did not hear about people flying the craft until 2013. But this reference in Steven's song goes back to 1972.

Wilson Leak Document

There is an interesting connection between the possible consciousness of the UFO and a document leaked into the UFO community a couple of years back.

The *Wilson Leak document* is a document that came from the files of the late Apollo 14 astronaut Dr. Edgar Mitchell. The document details the reported conversation between Dr. Eric Davis, a physicist then connected to the National Institute of Discovery Science (NIDS) run by Bob Bigelow, and the former head of Intelligence for the Joint Chiefs of Staff, Admiral Tom Wilson.[31]

The NIDS organization was busy trying to solve many of the UFO mysteries such as UFO sightings, black triangles, cattle mutilation, the validity of the Alien Autopsy video from 1995, and the Holloman Air Force Base rumored film showing a landing of a UFO at the base.

One of the things that interested NIDS was the story of Dr. Edgar Mitchell, Dr. Steven Greer, and Commander Will Miller going to the Pentagon to brief Wilson on CSETI and the groups' attempts to get disclosure from the US government on the UFO situation.

The meeting was supposed to have gone on for 45 minutes but really went on for hours. It only ended when Dr. Mitchell stated he had to go to New York City and so had to leave.

The Wilson Leaked document notes many things that Wilson told Davis about what he knew about the UFO coverup at his high level.

The item related to flying the saucer came when Wilson talked about a possible saucer in the government's custody.

Figure 4 Admiral Tom Wilson

"They had an intact craft," reads the document, that "they believed could fly." Those are critically important words.

They had an intact craft they believed they could fly, but it appears they had not. So why had they not flown the craft?

Logically, it would appear they couldn't fly the craft, or as Don Schmitt once said, they couldn't find the start button. Perhaps it had a consciousness interface? Perhaps they could not start the craft because someone has to become one with the craft.? I believe they needed a consciousness understanding of this, which they did not have.

Even the document hints at this as Wilson tells Davis they have made slow progress on back-engineering and the recovered hardware. However, the back-engineering is not as simple as breaking down the components to figure out how it works.

If the craft is alive and conscious, it may laugh at the efforts to get it turned on.

- They had (program manager talking) a craft – an intact craft they believed could fly (space? air? water? dimensions?)
- Was it from overseas or not?
- Said NO! Could not be – not possible!!
- Why, I asked – where did it come from?
- Program manager said they didn't know where it was from [they had some ideas on this] – it was technology that *was not of this Earth – not made by man – not by human hands*
- Said were trying to understand and exploit technology; their program was going on for years and years with very slow progress
- Agonizingly slow with little or no success – painful lack of collaboration to get help from outside community of experts and facilities to assist effort – must remain isolated and use own facilities and cleared personnel – tough environment to work – about 400-800 (bigot list count) workers varying in number with funding or personnel changes
- Miller questions asked:
  - o Roswell – craft/bodies/autopsies
  - o Holloman AFB Landing
  - o MJ-12 and leaked docs
  - o Zamora & Bentwaters, etc.
- They were mum – declined to discuss these
- TW threatened to go to SAPOC to complain, gain access to their program
- They said go ahead and do what you must
- I was angry because they defied my authority to be read-in with good logical reason – wouldn't budge
- Their tone was very testy/terse throughout conversation

EWD: What was outcome?

TW: Meeting broke up and I returned to Washington

EWD: What about Corso?

TW: Greer talked about Corso on April 9th
- Miller showed me the book during two-hour private conversation
- Didn't have time to read it through
- Didn't buy a copy
- Didn't bring Corso up at meeting
- But comparing Corso story to what I learned at meeting is more than enough to believe Corso told truth about seeing "alien" hardware, etc.

EWD: Did you complain to SAPOC?

TW: Yes – called the subgroup members (Senior Review Group members) to a meeting at Pentagon
- Told them what happened at meeting

13

DARPA and the FireFox

Figure 5 Dr. Eric Walker, former President at Penn State University and Chairman of the Board at the Institute for Defense Analysis, where DARPA originated.

In 1990, an interview took place between Henry Azadehdel and Dr. Eric Walker, the former president of Penn State University. More importantly, Walker was chairman of the board at the top military think tank for the United States government – the Institute for Defense Analysis. It was the institute for Defense Analysis that was given the job of setting up the Advanced Research Projects Agency (ARPA) after the

Sputnik disaster, which later became The Defense Advanced Research Projects Agency or DARPA.

Walker had been identified as a key figure in 1947 when the UFO cover-up began. He admitted the first time he was contacted that he had attended a series of briefings given to scientists and engineers at WPAFB (Wright Patterson Air Force Base) in 1950 on the results of a UFO crash.

In the interview, Azadehdel asks about the control group, and the following conversation led to the idea of non-local consciousness:

Dr. Walker: I cannot answer that. How good is your seventh sense? How much [do] you know about ESP?

Azadehdel: I know to some degree about ESP and EVP. But what has this got to do with it?

Dr. Walker: Unless you know about it and know how to use it, you would not be taken in. Only a few know about it.

Some people will be alarmed by stories of people flying saucers with their minds. Some may even suffer from cognitive dissonance as the discomfort of their beliefs clashes with this new information. This cognitive dissonance concept was proposed by Leon Festinger, who was studying a UFO cult that believed the end of the world was at hand.

When the events did not occur when predicted, Festinger noticed that the group went to the media and started proselytizing. They were seeking social support to lessen the pain. This can happen to conditioned minds that believe there are no UFOs, ETs, and the like.

In an endeavor to reduce their discomfort, such disbelievers will do everything in their power to resolve the contradiction and return the world to its former state.

This effort to return to internal psychological consistency usually involves allowing the left-brain interpreter (LBI) to handle the problem because that is its job. It is there to fill the holes that are created by new ideas in the established belief structure.

Research conducted by Dr. Michael Gazzaniga, University of California, Santa Barbara, in the 1970s and

1980s on the LBI showed that the LBI solves the dilemma by simply making up something. It confabulates; it lies to you. The research shown is almost always wrong, but it can hold its own in any debate because once the LBI makes up a story, it will stick to the story until death.

In the case of the people flying the saucer with consciousness, what will probably be thrown out by the LBI is that this is just an illusion (whatever that is), all the people are lying, and the evidence is just a collection of anecdotal stories, or it is pseudoscience. Some may simply utter the famous Stephen Hawking line "Nonsense."

The problem with these LBI creations is that people have been working on this problem for years, and there is evidence that the technology may be closer than one would think.

Firefox is a 1982 movie starring Clint Eastwood based on a 1977 book by the same name. In the film, Eastwood steals a fictional MiG-31 that bears a strong resemblance to an actual Soviet aircraft, The Tupolev Tu-144 supersonic airliner, nicknamed the "Konkordski" by the western aviation press. In the movie, Eastwood must use his mind to control the craft and escape with it. The plot sounds very much like the symbiotic relationship between the mind of the person piloting the UFO and the UFO itself.

As has been mentioned a couple of times in this book, the Canadians stated that the Americans knew about a mental connection to the flying saucers. It would be safe to assume then that they were thinking about a way to power the UFO with the mind and move that technology to operate other things like weapons and perhaps other world leaders.

It must be remembered that the famous MK-Ultra program, which had all sorts of secret programs to understand and control human consciousness, started only months after the Canadian memo about flying saucers and mental phenomena was written. The Canadian Defense Research Board (DRB) convened a secret meeting in Montreal attended by military officials from the United Kingdom, Canada, and two CIA officials. The focus of the meeting was — "Brainwashing Techniques."

More importantly, the Canadian representative at the meeting was Dr. Omand Solandt, who was involved in the UFO program and is even mentioned in the Wilbert Smith *Top-Secret memo* on UFOs.

Another indication that a human-machine interface was being actively studied came from the work of J.C.R. Licklider, which was published in 1960 called *Man-Computer Symbiosis*. In this paper, Licklider proposed:

> *...the development of man-computer symbiosis by analyzing some problems of interaction between men and computing machines, calling attention to applicable principles of man-machine engineering, and pointing out a few questions to which research answers are needed. In not too many years, the hope is that human brains and computing machines will be coupled together very tightly and that the resulting partnership will think as no human brain has ever thought and process data in a way not approached by the information-handling machines we know today.*

The movie plays off this idea of a brain-computer interface (BCI) or brain-machine interface (BMI.) This is a direct transmission pathway between the brain's electrical action and an external device, such as a plane. The most common use for brain interfaces today is a computer or robotic limb. However, this technology seems to be a few steps back from what people in this book describe as happening with the craft.

Research on BCIs began in the 1970s by Jacques Vidal at the University of California, Los Angeles (UCLA) under a grant from the National Science Foundation, followed by a contract from DARPA.

DARPA has always been tied to UFO technology. My friend Bob Emenegger once told a story of a tour through the military labs at DARPA, which indicated the military was involved in the race to link the mind to a machine. In one lab, the scientist refused to describe what he was doing until he was told by the official conducting the tour that he could describe what was going on. The man stated that he would sit on one side of the room, and a computer would sit on the other side of the room. The man would think of a word, and the computer would repeat the word without a physical interface. They were at the point where the computer could pick up almost ten words.

In 2019, an article was printed in *Live Science* that updated the DARPA efforts to understand and use consciousness:

> *DARPA, the Department of Defense's research arm, is paying scientists to invent ways to instantly read soldiers' minds using tools like genetic engineering of the human brain, nanotechnology, and infrared beams. The end goal? Thought-controlled weapons, like swarms of drones that someone sends to the skies with a single thought or the ability to beam images from one brain to another.*
>
> *This week, DARPA (Defense Advanced Research Projects Agency) announced that six teams will receive funding under the Next-Generation Nonsurgical Neurotechnology (N3) program. Participants are tasked with developing technology that will provide a two-way channel for rapid and seamless communication between the human brain and machines without requiring surgery.[32]*

Money has also gone into other studies that have gone public. For example, a neurologist at Duke University, Miguel Nicolelis, implanted electrodes into a monkey, allowing her to move a robot arm as if it were her own. She was then taught to move a cursor on a computer screen, and a robot arm in another room would award her with juice.

When the joystick was removed, the monkey did not know. So she continued moving it just by thinking.

This kind of research may have led to the 1977 Firefox book. The DARPA program was going in the 1970s, not long after reports of the secret stealth aircraft were leaking, and George Lawrence's biocybernetics program of "thought-controlled weapons" was starting to be written about.

Where did DARPA get the idea of using the mind to control things? It may have well been the UFO mental phenomena data that was already shared with the Canadians in 1950. It may have been UFO experiencers the government was aware of, just like those in this book. It may have been the work being done by the Soviets on the psychic phenomenon and mental influencing being done in the early 70s that led the American government to fund research into remote viewing.

The most dramatic technology I have seen in the white world tends to indicate that DARPA-type research in the black world might be very far along with flying a ship with the mind. The amazing white world technology goes all the way back to 2004.

The research was carried out by Thomas DeMarse, a biomedical engineer at the University of Florida in Gainesville.

DeMarse used 25,000 neutrons connected to 60 electrodes in a petri dish, neurons from a rat brain, to fly an F-22 fighter jet.

DeMarse first puts the neurons in the petri dish; they appear like individual cells mixed in water. In the first couple of days, however, individual neurons soon begin to extend microscopic lines toward each other, making connections that represent neural processes. "You see one extend a process, pull it back, extend it out — and it may do that a couple of times, just sampling who's next to it, until over time the connectivity starts to establish itself," DeMarse stated. "(The brain is) getting its network to the point where it's a live computation device."[33]

The *New Scientist* magazine described it this way:

> *Enzymes were used to extract neurons from the motor cortex of mature rat embryos, and cells were then seeded onto a grid of gold electrodes patterned on a glass Petri dish. The cells grew microscopic interconnections, turning them into*

a 'live computation device. DeMarse's array of 25,000 interconnected neurons were able to convert signals that indicated whether the simulated plane is experiencing stable conditions or hurricanes into a measurement of whether the plane is flying straight or tilted and then correct the flight path by transmitting signals to the airplane's controls.'[34]

the work has lost much of its initial WOW factor after people discovered that the rat brain did not teach itself and researchers were "manually tuning the weights between each of the nodes," but the concept remains.

How long will it be until objects are made with biological material that can be programmed? The same might apply to using bioboards for computers.

This is white-world technology that is almost 20 years old. I am sure it did not escape the eyes of biotech companies and scientists working in unacknowledged special access programs. One Reddit post seems to back this up, saying that some of DeMarse's research "got classified as it deals with autonomous flight control."

Artificial Intelligence

The other big takeaway from this book deals with the idea of artificial intelligence (AI). Experiencers clearly describe what appears to be artificial intelligence connected to the UFO intelligence.

The difference in their artificial intelligence is as follows:

- The modern concepts of AI consider consciousness as a physical thing like gravity or a box of nails. They view it as a process emerging from dead, unconscious matter. It arises when the system gets complex enough. It would be like the idea that if we keep piling rocks on each other, it will eventually produce consciousness. In this model, we figure out what the conscious is, capture it, and add it to our technology and toys.
- What the experiencers in this book are reporting is something different. Consciousness is primary, and matter arises from consciousness. Higher, more complex consciousness is tied to biological systems. The experiencers in this book describe the crafts as being biological – alive. The consciousness was not put into the metal. Everything on the ship is alive. It is true artificial intelligence is based on creating things with biological systems and principles.
- Not discussed in this book is another AI repeatedly reported by anyone who has experienced the greys. Witnesses will maintain that the small 3–4-foot worker greys are robotic, and all look the same, as though they were created in molds. It is quite conservable that they, like the ship, have been created by manipulating biological material to produce a being that does nothing but picks up and takes experiencers back to

their bedrooms. Unlike the *2001 A Space Odyssey* rebellious AI computer known as HAL, these AI greys are under total control by the tall greys reported on the ship.

Final Thoughts

Form follows Consciousness. Human Form follows human consciousness. Our minds create our bodies. Not the other way around.
-Dr. Rebecca Hardcastle Wright

It is not altogether clear to me why we have become so attached to our way of seeing the world. Perhaps a comprehensive scientific paradigm gives a sense of mastery and power... This might be why it is the intellectual and political elite in our culture that seem most deeply wedded to perpetrating the materialistic view of reality.
-Dr. John Mack

"Most physicists develop a somewhat schizophrenic view. On the one hand, they accept the standard interpretation of the quantum theory, including the epistemological irreducibility of the system and observer. On the other, they insist on the reality of quantum systems even when these are not observed."
-Dr. Fritz Rohrlich of Syracuse University

As Cat Stevens and every other Sky Pilot witness I have talked to in this book describe, there is no steering wheel on a UFO.

The other thing that I have noticed is that usually, people only have one incident where they fly the craft. I have never heard anyone tell me that they remember several training sessions. They appear once and seem to know what to do. They do it, and often that is the last time it happens.

The whole process is centered around what Dr. Eric Walker described as the 7th sense. "Unless you understand this, you will not be taken in. Very few people understand."

We are very far from understanding this mental aspect of the world, sometimes referred to as the hard problem of consciousness. It is complex now, and our understanding is still years away in the future.

That is also a point that Dr. Walker made in his early 1990s discussions, "Unless you have the mind of Einstein," he stated, "you will not get anywhere."

Dr. Eric Davis, an astrophysicist who has worked on the UFO problem for 30 years, stated that the government had not made much progress in back-engineering the crafts. That was supported by the statement of three experts who met in a Denny's restaurant in the 1980s to discuss "What do we really know about UFOs?" given all the crazy stuff that researchers were putting out. They claimed in their conclusion that there are visitors of some sort, they have left hardware on Earth, and we have not been able to back-engineer it.

Jim Semivan, a former high-level CIA official who encountered the UFO intelligence one night in his bedroom, stated, "This is an incredibly complex topic. I don't think they're going to come up with any answers at all, and I don't even know if they're going to come up with a direction to take."

The world is dominated by materialistic thinking, so perhaps everyone is still running down the wrong research roads. This is not aided by the fact that extremely Top-Secret programs are highly compartmentalized, so everyone has only a tiny piece of the puzzle.

Looking at experiencer reports provides other hints that mental phenomena is the most critical aspect of this, as the Canadians in 1950 described it. For example, I have heard a few stories of children on board ships, such as one told to me by Pam DuPuis.

In this story, children are seated in a circle. Someone is instructing them, but they cannot see above the waist. As the story goes, the children are being taught to levitate balls of three different colors. The one-colored ball is very easy to move. The second color ball is harder, and the third color is a real challenge. They are playing a game where they are levitating the balls from one to another.

One reason that the entities are training people to fly craft doesn't appear to be war. There has never been an experiencer who was told they were part of an alien invasion that some researchers constantly want to warn about.

What differs between these experiencer pilots from our military pilots is that military pilots are raised and trained in a belief of separation. In our military pilot world, we are the good guy, and then there are the bad guys.

The planes and the pilots that fly them have changed the nature and brutality of war.

In the days before flight, armies would line up against each other on the battlefield and kill each other. Only the people in the battle would suffer and die.

Once the plane was invented, it suddenly became possible to drop bombs from planes. These would be dropped on troop positions, but that was accelerated by dropping bombs on innocent civilians to pressure the government to change policy or surrender.

In the world of separation, only the self is important. Those on the other side, whether man, woman, or child, become the enemy, and their deaths become collateral damage or a necessary cost of war.

We dropped bombs and killed millions of innocent civilians in World War II. We dropped two atomic bombs that ended the lives of over 100,000 civilians just living to have a good life. We firebombed 63 cities in Japan in World War II that cremated 1,000,000 people alive in 1,500-degree temperatures. The list goes on and on.

Many UFO researchers and ex-government officials continue to push the UAP threat scenario, but it is not the UAP pilots that are dropping the bombs. Whenever they push me on the threat issue, I say, "When they drop the first atomic bomb, send me the evil alien petition. Until then, we have met the enemy, and he is us."

Figure 6 Children growing up in the rubble of World War II. The damage was done by the planes above.

The people on board the ships report the #1 message is Oneness. This is the concept that everyone is part of the same whole. So, therefore, why would someone drop a bomb on themselves?

Those who control the best available evidence may cover this aspect of the UFO story. However, if they put out the fact that we should live and act as one, where does that leave the 700+ billion dollars national insecurity budget that pays their salaries? There is not much war and profit in the idea that we are all cells in the same body.

Time and Space

Time and space are modes by which we think and not conditions in which we live.
-Albert Einstein

"Wherever I put my mind I could go. Time and space had vanished for me. I could be anywhere at any time." Saw dog at the end of the street and was instantly there. Saw tree and was instantly there. NASA Biological Oceanographer Ingrid Honkala talking about her near-death-experience.

The biggest lesson from all the people who have flown the craft is the idea that what is happening may be signaling a new understanding of reality, especially when it comes to time and space. As in other books detailing reports from experiencers, space and time collapse, or they are nonrelevant. People describe being in multiple places at the same time.

Many of the subjects in this book described how their travel *out there* was almost instantaneous. If that description is accurate, it doesn't take a genius to figure out we may not fully understand what space is.

Ron Johnson was asked where he wanted to go and said he wanted to see the milky way from a distance. So, in one second, he could see the milky way in the distance.

Kevin Briggs described that his travels to other star systems were immediate.

Jean Kimura stated that she was told to visualize where she wanted to go and then push the button. She did, and she was there. She could never get over how fast it happened.

Desta's account was the same; once she decided where she wanted to go, she was there instantly.

Chris Bledsoe described in his 2007 abduction experience how time was quite different. He was reported missing for 4.5 hours, yet on board the ship, the time was different. "Egypt is the centerpiece of what happened in 2007. They took me for four and a half hours. That four and a half hours seemed like four and a half months."[35]

Skeptics would say that Chris imagined that, but it is just as valid to say that it was the real-time, and the four and a half hours were the fantasy. We know from NDEs, OBEs, and abduction experiencers that the witnesses, who are the only people who have had both experiences of time, will say that the waking state is actually the dream and that the non-local experience was more real than the real world.

The Edgar Mitchell FREE survey of people claiming they had encounters with non-human intelligences backs up Bledsoe's story. Answering the question, "In this 'matrix' reality, did you perceive that time did not exist?" And 70.9% of the respondents answered Yes.

There are also well-known cases in the world regarding DMT trips. For example, in the documentary *The Spirit Molecule*, one person stated he believed that he had lived 1,000 years when the experience was over in ten minutes in our present-day, conscious reality. Another report had the witness state that he had been gone 2,500 years.

It is evident time may not really exist. Einstein said, "Time and space are modes by which we think and not conditions in which we live," and "The distinction between the past, present, and future is only a stubbornly persistent illusion."

The same thing applies to space. Those who flew the craft reported almost instantaneous movement to places light-years away in a second. This would strongly indicate that the stars and planet may not be way out there. "Quantum physics thus reveals a basic oneness of the universe," wrote quantum pioneer Erwin Schrodinger.

This potential lack of space was also evident in the remote viewing work done by the United States government, where people were remote sensing or going out of their bodies to see things anywhere in time and space. As one of the two directors of the CIA program, Dr. Russel Targ, stated, it is as easy to remote view in the past and future as it is in the present moment, and it is as easy to remote view on the other side of the world as it is in the next room.

As mentioned earlier, prominent physicist John Wheeler stated, "There is no out there out there" and that "It's a participatory universe."

Everything that happens does so in our minds, and scientists can't even find where that mind or conscious awareness is.

Deepak Chopra defined it the best, saying, "Everything is an activity inside consciousness, and everyday reality is a projection of a more fundamental reality."

The universe out there may be something strictly inside our awareness, like a virtual reality game or a simulated universe.

This agrees with some of the early founders of quantum mechanics (QM), like Max Planck, who said, "I regard consciousness as fundamental. I regard matter as derivative from consciousness. We cannot get behind consciousness. Everything that we talk about, everything that we regard as existing, postulates consciousness."

It sounds far-out but consider what many UFO experiencers, like Ron Johnson, Chris Bledsoe, and Terry Lovelace, reported. The inside of the craft is way bigger than the outside. One client of Dr. John Mack at Harvard University described the size of the inside of a small craft as the size of Fenway Park.

This material worldview is not possible, but there are scores of stories describing this bizarre characteristic of the insides of the ships. If the physical world of time and space were real, this would not be happening.

This time-space dilemma may be critical to understanding where the intelligence comes from and how they get here. If time and space don't really exist and there is only the here and now, how big is the here and now? It would have to be a singularity that perceives size and time. And with no space, it would have to be nothing more than a one-dimensional point in space.[2]

How long would it take to cross a point in space? The answer may be that they have always been here, as they have told many experiencers, and we all live in the same point of here and now.

The Simulated Universe and Maya

The spirit is the life. The mind is the builder, and the
physical is the result.
-Edgar Cayce

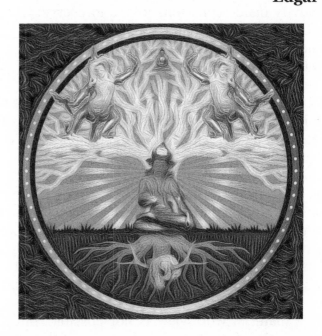

---

[2] The 2022 Nobel Prize was given to three researchers who proved the fact that spooky action at a distance does exist and has been confirmed in laboratories.

As early QM (Quantum Mechanic) practitioners established, consciousness is primary. It creates matter – not the other way around. And with recent discoveries, the waking reality looks more and more like a subset of a greater reality that is much more plastic and much more like the experiences people are reporting in contact with the intelligence behind the UFO phenomenon.

Suppose reality is based on consciousness resembling a modern video game. In that case, the idea of conscious crafts being flown around by conscious beings instantaneously from one point in the universe to another starts to sound possible. All that is required is dropping the mistaken ideas we have been programmed with inside the conditioned mind, making it all seem impossible.

Anil Seth, professor of neuroscience at the University of Sussex in the U.K., spelled out the situation as follows, "Our conscious experiences of the world around us, and of ourselves within it, are kinds of controlled hallucinations that happen with, through, and because of our living bodies."

This all seemed to be the talk of crazy people. Even 20 years ago, raising the subject of consciousness in academia was a good reason for ex-communication. Now it seems to be all the rage. However, most are still stuck in a materialistic dogma, so consciousness research is generally restricted to discovering the biological basis of consciousness. This leads to a worldview where almost all consciousness research has the underlying belief that there is a football game inside of the TV and that Elvis is still alive and singing inside of radios around the world.

The modern research that is starting to shake these faith-based beliefs is the theoretical research and discussion dealing with the simulated reality that was brought into the modern zeitgeist by video games, virtual reality, and the movie *The Matrix*.

The technology of virtual reality is becoming so good that it is starting to rival waking reality. Scientists and computer people started to hypothesize that computers could simulate reality to a degree indistinguishable from our "true" reality. It could contain conscious minds that may or may not know that they live inside a simulation.

The new concept is strikingly similar to the Eastern concept of MAYA, considered the one true reality. Maya in Sanskrit means magic or illusion. This fundamental Hindu concept, most notably in the Advaita (Nondualist) school of Vedanta, is basically the simulated universe theory that has become popular in the west.

The difference is that in the West, the belief is that there may be some master computer programmer running the game, whereas, in Vedanta, all is an illusion made from vibrating consciousness or Source. It is "a play of the supreme consciousness of God." In such a world, there are no nouns. There is just one thing - Source. It is alive. It is a verb, not a noun.

In such a world, God did not create the heavens and Earth. This is the idea that God creates the physical heavens and Earth. Then he created man and stuck a soul (consciousness) in him.

The concept of Maya specifies that there is no physical world. It indicates that the supreme consciousness, or the ONE, created sparks of the divine to go out and create our experience. The sparks are the ones that created the heavens and Earth. This model lines up with the observer effect, or the idea that matter does not come into existence until there is an observer. We, the observers, **are** the sparks, and we are creating the physical and other worlds with their awareness.

Marc Leavitt is a researcher who has written four books based on his search on the topic of reality. He became an active meditation practitioner and is on a quest to understand ultimate reality. One trip he had contained visions he experienced after returning home from a course at the Monroe Institute. He called it the *Grand Design of Creation*.

Like other Eastern mystics, he concluded that we project reality from our awareness. As he described, our faces are jammed up against a movie screen, and we think we are in the movie.

In another vision, he was told to look behind himself; what he saw was the void or the nothing. As he turned back, he saw that the screen of reality was moved back, and he could see it was just a projection. He looked the other way, and there was the void. He saw that he was stuck between the two. Because the screen had been moved back a couple of feet, he could see the actual reality that it was a projection, and his awareness was the projector.

The scientific version of this idea in science was expressed by Dr. Max Planck, the father of quantum physics:

> *As a man who has devoted his whole life to the most clearheaded science, to the study of matter, I can tell you as a result of my research about the atoms this much: There is no matter as such! All matter originates and exists only by virtue of a force which brings the particles of an atom to vibration and holds this most minute solar system of the atom together... We must assume behind this force the existence of a conscious and intelligent Mind. This Mind is the matrix of all matter.*

The 5,000-year-old eastern concept of Maya was defended earlier by the first scientist Rene Descartes who coincidentally came up with the scientific method when it came to him one night in a dream:

> *But I cannot forget that at other times I have been deceived in sleep by similar illusions; and, attentively considering those cases, I perceive so clearly that there exist no certain marks by which the state of waking can ever be distinguished from sleep, that I feel greatly astonished. In amazement, I almost persuade myself that I am now dreaming... How can you be certain that your whole life is not a dream?*

In the 21st century, people like MIT computer scientist and Silicon Valley video game designer Rizwan Virk have now supported the Maya nondual concept. Rizwan wrote the book the *Simulated Universe*. In the book, he looks at the scientific, religious, and mystical to explore the possibility of a reality different from what you know to be real.

Michael Talbot, a UFO experiencer and client of Budd Hopkins, wrote a book called *The Holographic Universe.* In it, he investigated evidence that the universe may be one giant hologram, not the nuts-and-bolts random world we have been programmed to believe. Talbot wrote:

> *Was it possible, he wondered, that what the mystics had been saying for centuries was true, reality was Maya, an illusion. And what was out there was really a vast, resonating symphony of waveforms, a 'frequency domain' that was transformed into the world as we know it only after it entered our senses?*

Apollo 14 astronaut Dr. Edgard Mitchell would also conclude this evidenced by his writing a whole book on the quantum hologram. Later, he would apply this model of reality by conducting a major study on UFO experiencers, looking at the supporting evidence these people were getting from non-human intelligences.

Then, a cognitive scientist at the University of California, Irvine, Dr. Donald Hoffman, joined in with his book *The Case Against Reality: Why Evolution Hid the Truth from Our Eyes.*

Hoffman is exceptionally significant in that part of his biography was working for Dr. Francis Crick, one of the two men who discovered the helical structure of DNA. Crick maintained, "You're nothing but a pack of neurons." Hoffman tasked Crick with finding consciousness in the brain. After decades he gave up and adopted more of a simulated universe theory.

Hoffman argues against the leading scientific theories claiming that our senses report objective reality. He maintains that while we should take our perceptions seriously, we should not take them literally. He maintains that everything we see in the physical world is like a desktop icon, not actual reality. This implies that the world we see is not an objective reality.

Atlantic Magazine described Hoffman as the man who was trying to discover the reality behind the illusion.

Finally, there is Dr. Robert Lanza, one of the top scientists in the United States, who argues that consciousness is the driving force in the creation of the universe.

In a new paper published in the *Journal of Cosmology and Astroparticle Physics,* Lanza questioned, "Is there a physical reality that is independent of us? Does objective reality exist at all? Or is the structure of everything, including time and space, created by the perceptions of those observing it?"

In his two books, *Biocentrism* and *Beyond Biocentrism,* Lanza spells out his research that illustrates that the physical world that we perceive is not something separate from us but is created by our minds as we observe it. Time and space are simply a byproduct of the "whirl of information" in our heads that we weave together with our minds into a coherent experience.

This is pretty much what Jean Kimura was told by the alien when she asked how she could fly the ship anywhere she wanted to go. He said, "You must see it in your mind." When she did, she was there instantly.

It is also described by people like Father Nathan Castle, who has worked with dying people to help them cross over but who get "stuck" and cannot move into the next state. He has documented 400 cases in the last 23 years and has produced a predictable pattern.

The post-death world he describes is very much like the world where people are flying crafts with their intention. However, it is also like the lucid dream world where the environment is very plastic and instantly changeable.

In the lucid dream world, once the person realizes they are inside a dream, they can change the characters in the dream and move around instantly, just like the UFO sky pilots.

The same rule seems to apply to remote viewing. Not only can the mind go wherever it wants in whatever time period, but it can also instantly know what the target is even though the conscious mind is blinded to what the target is. It is as if everything is here and now with no time or space and that everything is within and instantly accessible.

This may be what Dr. John Wheeler hinted at when he said there is no out there, out there.

The clients of Father Castle basically describe the same nonlocal world where what they think about manifests almost instantly. So it is further evidence of the observer effect in quantum mechanics that there may not be an "independent world out there" but rather a world that comes into reality within the person's mind.

In most cases, Father Castle will bring in another deceased person to help the dying person move on. Some of these include Einstein, Jesus, and a baseball player named Lou Gehrig. These people seem to instantly manifest, like the craft moving light-years in seconds. As Castle points out, other things like equipment can be brought in. Consider this case: the guy involved became known as the conductor.

Castle dreamt about cars being hit at a rail crossing without a gate or a warning signal. Sometimes he could see people there, and sometimes he could not. When he awoke from this dream, he believed this accident would involve multiple people.[3]

Later, when he and his prayer partner (his sister in this case) made contact, they encountered a man who said he had been a passenger in a car where they had been out having a good time, which implied drinking. The car he was in was hit by a train at a crossing.

This man had a bit of an attitude and wouldn't tell Father Nathan his name. He just said to call me "Buddy." He didn't want to be friendly. He just was here to do this getting unstuck thing. He had been sent to Father Nathan by his guides, who had done their best. Buddy said his guides said he was to be the conductor. He was upset and said, "I am not a conductor. I never said I was a conductor."

Father Nathan said, 'OK, well, tell us what happened and where you are."

---

[3] Father Nathan believes that people will sometimes cluster in the afterlife based on how they died. In this case a bunch of people theoretically had been hit by trains and were stuck in their crossing over.

UFO Sky Pilots

The guy explained that a train track ran through where the people were stuck in this place where all these spirits were stuck. He said there was a boulder on the track, and they could not get out.

Father Nathan said, "Well, that sounds like you are stuck, and I believe you are here with me because we are supposed to help you find a way out. So let's get to work. Do you have a fulcrum, like some stick that you could use, or could all the people throw their weight against it to move it?"

Buddy replied, "It would be easier if we had some heavy equipment."

Father said, "That would be much better than my way. Have you asked for it?"

Buddy said, "No."

Father Nathan said, "Well, let's start there. Let's ask for some heavy equipment. I'm a priest, so I am going to say a prayer (comparable to the idea of intention in mystical literature). Would it be alright if I asked for heavy equipment?"

Buddy said, "Well, be sure to ask for the key for the ignition."

Father Nathan said, "Well, if I am asking for the key to the ignition, maybe I should ask for a heavy equipment operator just in case it is more difficult to operate than you are able to do."

Buddy said, "Sure, that's alright."

Father Nathan prayed for the piece of heavy equipment, the key, and the operator.

Within 10 seconds, Buddy said, "Oh my God, look over there."

Father Nathan said, "I can't see whatever you are seeing. What is it?"

Buddy replied, "It's like a front-end loader."

Father Nathan asked, "Is it yellow?"

Buddy replied, "Yeah, it is, and there's a guy in it who's waving for me to come up in the cab with him."

Father Nathan asked him if he thought he was being tricked. Did he think it would be safe to do it?

165

Buddy said, "No, it's okay. I'm going to do it." So he got up in it and got to the controls.

As he did, he said, "Oh my God, look at that."

Father Nathan reminded him he could not see what Buddy was viewing.

Buddy said, 'There is a great big bubble, and there are people in it, and one of them is my papa."

Nathan asked him if he looked scary, to which Buddy replied, "No, he just looks like my papa."

Nathan said, "Well, it looks like he has come to help you."

Buddy said, "They are saying that I am supposed to get everyone that wants to join hands, and we will go together. " They would join hands and all push and go together, and that's the way it worked. Nathan told him to tell them, "All aboard. You need to get all these people holding hands and lining up."

Off they went.

Just before Buddy left, he said, "I thought I was the last person who would be a conductor of anything." He was only 20 years old when he died and had not done well in school. He felt he wasn't much good at anything.

The story's point is that in the matrix land of the dead or UFO intelligence, the mind seems to be the builder, and manifesting is much easier to do than in the physical world.

Once again, the skeptics will say, "This is all nonsense, illusion, and pseudoscience. I know, and you just believe."

I would remind them that the skeptics have always been wrong, whether it be defending the flat earth, the sun going around the Earth, being at the center of the universe, things being solid, everything in physics being discovered in 1874, flight being impossible, going past the speed of sound being impossible, defending the idea that there is only one galaxy, everything is solid, there are no UFOs, etc.

I will close on a positive note. Believing that there is more than the material world has always been an excellent way to lose an academic job, not get promoted, or lose all possible funding. However, things are changing, and many of the concepts written in this book will be validated one day, just as I said in 1975, that UFOs are real. I listened to skeptics for decades, and they were wrong. I was right.

I said in 2012 that consciousness would be the key to the UFO mystery, and even fellow researchers tried to throw me to the wolves. However, there has been a big movement on the subject of consciousness, and it is now a big buzzword in Ufology. Even people who do not have a clue about consciousness are using the word.

A few years back, a movement began to move science and research into a post-materialist world. What resulted was *The Manifesto for Post-Materialist Science*. It was prepared by Mario Beauregard, Ph.D. (University of Arizona), Gary E. Schwartz, Ph.D. (University of Arizona), and Lisa Miller, Ph.D. (Columbia University), in collaboration with Larry Dossey, MD, Alexander Moreira-Almeida, MD, Ph.D., Marilyn Schlitz, Ph.D., Rupert Sheldrake, Ph.D., and Charles Tart, Ph.D.

Since it was written, over 450 academics (professors, M.D. s, and scientists) have signed the manifesto. There will be many more coming, as the *New York Times* December 2017 UFO article showed that there is a big gap in our understanding of reality and that we are no longer at the top of the intellectual food chain in the Universe.

Realizing that new technology and Nobel Prizes are waiting for those who wade into paranormal research, many younger open-minded scientists are taking up the challenge. For example, *the Galileo Project*, run out of Harvard looking at the UFO issue, had over 100 academics who joined a Manhattan-type effort to figure out what is going on.

Paranormal issues such as Skinwalker Ranch or UFOs can now be talked about in academic facilities and even in the halls of the Pentagon. Everyone is out of the closet, and the race for understanding has begun.

Here is the wording of the *Post Materialistic Science Manifesto* posted at Openscience.org[36]:

We believe that the sciences are being constricted by dogmatism, and in particular by a subservience to the philosophy of materialism,

> *the doctrine that matter is the only reality and that the mind is nothing but the physical activity of the brain. We believe that the sciences would be more scientific if they were free to investigate the natural world in a truly open way – without the constraints of materialism and the prejudice of dogma – while adhering to the scientific methods of data collecting, hypothesis testing, and critical discussion.*

1. The modern scientific worldview is predominantly predicated on assumptions that are closely associated with classical physics. Materialism—the idea that matter is the only reality—is one of these assumptions. A related assumption is reductionism, the notion that complex things can be understood by reducing them to the interactions of their parts or to simpler or more fundamental things such as tiny material particles.
2. During the 19th century, these assumptions narrowed, turned into dogmas, and coalesced into an ideological belief system that came to be known as "scientific materialism." This belief system implies that the mind is nothing but the physical activity of the brain and that our thoughts cannot have any effect on our brains and bodies, our actions, and the physical world.
3. The ideology of scientific materialism became dominant in academia during the 20th century. So dominant that a majority of scientists started to believe that it was based on established empirical evidence and represented the only rational view of the world.
4. Scientific methods based upon materialistic philosophy have been highly successful in increasing our understanding of nature and bringing greater control and freedom through advances in technology.
5. However, the nearly absolute dominance of materialism in the academic world has seriously constricted the sciences and hampered the development of the scientific study of mind and

spirituality. Faith in this ideology, as an exclusive explanatory framework for reality, has compelled scientists to neglect the subjective dimension of human experience. This has led to a severely distorted and impoverished understanding of ourselves and our place in nature.

6. Science is, first and foremost, a non-dogmatic, open-minded method of acquiring knowledge about nature through observation, experimental investigation, and theoretical explanation of phenomena. Its methodology is not synonymous with materialism and should not be committed to any particular beliefs, dogmas, or ideologies.

7. At the end of the nineteenth century, physicists discovered empirical phenomena that classical physics could not explain. During the 1920s and early 1930s, this led to the development of a revolutionary new branch of physics called quantum mechanics (QM). QM has questioned the material foundations of the world by showing that atoms and subatomic particles are not really solid objects—they do not exist with certainty at definite spatial locations and definite times. Most importantly, QM explicitly introduced the mind into its basic conceptual structure since it was found that the particles being observed and the observer—the physicist and the method used for observation—are linked. According to one interpretation of QM, this phenomenon implies that the consciousness of the observer is vital to the existence of the physical events being observed and that mental events can affect the physical world. The results of recent experiments support this interpretation. These results suggest that the physical world is no longer the primary or sole component of reality and that it cannot be fully understood without making reference to the mind.

8. Psychological studies have shown that conscious mental activity can causally influence behavior and that the explanatory and predictive value of agentic

factors (e.g., beliefs, goals, desires, and expectations) is very high. Moreover, research in psychoneuroimmunology indicates that our thoughts and emotions can markedly affect the activity of the physiological systems (e.g., immune, endocrine, and cardiovascular) connected to the brain. In other respects, neuroimaging studies of emotional self-regulation, psychotherapy, and the placebo effect demonstrate that mental events significantly influence the activity of the brain.

9. Studies of the so-called "psi phenomena" indicate that we can sometimes receive meaningful information without the use of ordinary senses and in ways that transcend the habitual space and time constraints. Furthermore, psi research demonstrates that we can mentally influence—at a distance—physical devices and living organisms (including other human beings). Psi research also shows that distant minds may behave in ways that are nonlocally correlated, i.e., the correlations between distant minds are hypothesized to be unmediated (they are not linked to any known energetic signal), unmitigated (they do not degrade with increasing distance), and immediate (they appear to be simultaneous). These events are so common that they cannot be viewed as anomalous nor as exceptions to natural laws but as indications of the need for a broader explanatory framework that cannot be predicated exclusively on materialism.

10. Conscious mental activity can be experienced in clinical death during a cardiac arrest (this is what has been called a "near-death experience" [NDE]). Some near-death experiencers (NDErs) have reported veridical out-of-body perceptions (i.e., perceptions that can be proven to coincide with reality) that occurred during cardiac arrest. NDErs also report profound spiritual experiences during NDEs triggered by cardiac arrest. It is noteworthy that the brain's electrical activity ceases within a few seconds following a cardiac arrest.

11. Controlled laboratory experiments have documented that skilled research mediums (people who claim they can communicate with the minds of people who have physically died) can sometimes obtain highly accurate information about deceased individuals. This further supports the conclusion that the mind can exist separate from the brain.

12. Some materialistically inclined scientists and philosophers refuse to acknowledge these phenomena because they are not consistent with their exclusive world conception. Rejection of post-materialist investigation of nature or refusal to publish strong scientific findings supporting a post-materialist framework is antithetical to the true spirit of scientific inquiry, which is that empirical data must always be adequately dealt with. Data that do not fit favored theories and beliefs cannot be dismissed a priori. Such dismissal is the realm of ideology, not science.

13. It is important to realize that psi phenomena, NDEs in cardiac arrest, and replicable evidence from credible research mediums appear anomalous only when seen through the lens of materialism.

14. Moreover, materialist theories fail to elucidate how the brain could generate the mind, and they are unable to account for the empirical evidence alluded to in this manifesto. This failure tells us that it is now time to free ourselves from the shackles and blinders of the old materialist ideology, enlarge our concept of the natural world, and embrace a post-materialist paradigm.

15. According to the post-materialist paradigm:

a. Mind represents an aspect of reality as primordial as the physical world. Mind is fundamental in the universe, i.e., it cannot be derived from matter and reduced to anything more basic.

b. There is a deep interconnectedness between the mind and the physical world.

c. Mind (will/intention) can influence the state of the physical world and operate in a nonlocal (or extended) fashion, i.e., it is not confined to specific points in space, such as brains and bodies, nor to specific points in time, such as the present. Since the mind may nonlocally influence the physical world, the intentions, emotions, and desires of an experimenter may not be completely isolated from experimental outcomes, even in controlled and blinded experimental designs.

d. Minds are apparently unbounded and may unite in ways suggesting a unitary, One Mind that includes all individual, single minds.

e. NDEs in cardiac arrest suggest that the brain acts as a transceiver of mental activity, i.e., the mind can work through the brain but is not produced by it. NDEs occurring in cardiac arrest, coupled with evidence from research mediums, further suggest the survival of consciousness following bodily death and the existence of other non-physical levels of reality.

f. Scientists should not be afraid to investigate spirituality and spiritual experiences since they represent a central aspect of human existence.

16. Post-materialist science does not reject empirical observations, and the great value of scientific achievements has been realized up until now. Instead, it seeks to expand the human capacity to understand the wonders of nature better and, in the process, rediscover the importance of mind and spirit as being part of the core fabric of the universe. Post-materialism includes matter, which is seen as a basic constituent of the universe.

17. The post-materialist paradigm has far-reaching implications. It fundamentally alters our vision of ourselves, giving us back our dignity and power as humans and as scientists. This paradigm fosters positive values such as compassion, respect, and peace. By emphasizing a deep connection between ourselves and nature at large, the post-materialist paradigm also promotes environmental awareness and the preservation of our biosphere. In addition, it is not new but only forgotten for four hundred years that a lived transmaterial understanding may be the cornerstone

of health and wellness, as it has been held and preserved in ancient mind-body-spirit practices, religious traditions, and contemplative approaches.

18. The shift from materialist science to post-materialist science may be of vital importance to the evolution of human civilization. It may be even more pivotal than the transition from geocentrism to heliocentrism.

Endnotes

¹https://bdigital.ufp.pt/bitstream/10284/781/1/223-239Cons-Ciencias%2002-8.pdf

² Corso, Col. Philip J., with Birnes, William J., The Day After Roswell, Pocket Books, New York and London, 1997, p. 90. Copyright © 1997 by Rosewood Woods Productions, Inc.

³ Ibid. Page 98

⁴ Castillo Rincón, Enrique, UFOs: A Great New Dawn for Humanity, Blue Dolphin Publishing, PO Box 8, Nevada City, California 95959, USA, 1997, (ISBN 1–57733–000–5) translated by Hugo A. Castro from the Spanish original edition, OVNI: Gran Alborada Humana, published by Enrique Castillo Rincón, San José, Costa Rica, 1995.

⁵ Ibid.

⁶ Timothy Good, "Unearthly Disclosure," https://avalonlibrary.net/ebooks/Timothy%20Good%20-%20Unearthly%20Disclosure.pdf

⁷ UFOs: A Great Dawn for Humanity, Page 66.

⁸ "The Alien Autopsy......Oh No Not Again!" https://personalpages.manchester.ac.uk/staff/neil.morris/Alien-Autopsy-Revisited.pdf

⁹ https://avalonlibrary.net/ebooks/Timothy%20Good%20-%20Unearthly%20Disclosure.pdf

¹⁰ "Garry Nolan: UFOs and Aliens | Lex Fridman Podcast #262," https://www.youtube.com/watch?v=uTCc2-1tbBQ

¹¹ GRANT CAMERON with Kevin Briggs on Apports, Nukes, Psychic Abilities and Channeling., https://www.youtube.com/watch?v=vuT_3MIR2Yw&t=3312s

¹² Grant Cameron Guest Rebecca Hardcastle Wright PhD on Meta-materials, Unified Fields, Exopolitics, https://www.youtube.com/watch?v=WL9YGpea6aY

¹³ https://anchor.fm/grant-cameron5/episodes/Episode-2---UFO-Portals-and-Flying-the-Craft-Interview-with-Captain-Joe-Vallejo-eteoom

14 Whitley Strieber interview of John Ramirez, "Dreamland Podcast," February 11, 2022.

15 Marcus Lowth, "The Alien Abduction Encounters Of Denise Stoner – A Lifetime Of Otherworldly Visitation," https://www.ufoinsight.com/aliens/abductions/alien-abduction-encounters-of-denise-stoner

16 "Consciousness," http://pathoftheshaballa.blogspot.com/2021/

17 Grant Cameron interview with Don Anderson, February 11, 2022.

18 https://anchor.fm/grant-cameron5/episodes/UFO-Propulsion-Japanese-MUFON-Director-Flies-the-UFO-The-Latest-of-over-four-Dozen-People-reporting-this-e1cavnd

19 Grant Cameron interview of Wendy Gallant "Wendy Gallant talks about visual lucidity, ET Encounters, and Flying the UFO," April 8, 2021.

20 Youtube Interview, August 3, 2020, "GRANT CAMERON ET Classrooms, Telepathy and Contact with Tress Hyde"

21 GRANT CAMERON on Abductions, Regressions and Screen Images with Candice Powers, https://www.youtube.com/watch?v=QAJxfUrTG18&t=1865s

22 Gary Nolan on the Evidence behind UFOs, Psychedelics and Artificial Consciousness, Host Curt Jaimungal, Podcast Theories of Everything.

23 https://studio.youtube.com/video/fQwrLXU1obg/edit

24 Ibid.

25 Ibid page 621.

26 Researcher Joe Murgia in his internet blog Joe Murgia, "Kit Green's Most Trusted Psychic: "The Disclosure Of Alien Presence Will Take Place This Way" told of being contacted by an anonymous source who had seen a few of (his) comments on Reddit in one of the UFO groups." This source provided Murgia an audio and transcript. I too received an audio and transcript to post on the internet and I believe the source of both transcripts appeared to be Dr. Ron Pandolfi.

I believe that Pandolfi may have gotten the audio tape from me as I provided it to someone who knew Pandolfi a few years back (minus a transcript). The transcript I received is identical to the one that Murgia posted. I have no idea who did the transcript.

27 VERONICA PAZ WELLS, "SOWERS OF LIFE," http://www.myshambhala.com/books/ufo/sunesis_project/Sowers_of_Life.pdf PAGE 71

28 RICARDO GONZÁLEZ, "CONTACT FROM APU," LUMINOUS MOON PRESS, PAGE 145

29 RICARDO GONZÁLEZ, "PHYSICAL ENCOUNTER AT MOUNT SHASTA, AUGUST 26, 2012, http://www.exopoliticsjournal.com/vol-4/vol-4-2-Gonzalez.htm

30 Grant Cameron, "Tuned In: The Paranormal World of Music," Page 152

31 https://www.documentcloud.org/documents/6185702-Eric-Davis-meeting-with-Adm-Wilson

[32] "The Government Is Serious About Creating Mind-Controlled Weapons," https://www.livescience.com/65546-darpa-mind-controlled-weapons.html

[33] ""Brain" In A Dish Acts As Autopilot Living Computer," https://research.ufl.edu/publications/explore/v10n1/extract2.html

[34] "Brain cells in a dish fly fighter plane." https://www.newscientist.com/article/dn6573-brain-cells-in-a-dish-fly-fighter-plane/#ixzz7K3dsU8V8

[35] Chris Bledsoe interview, "Bledsoe Said So Podcast" Bledsoe Said So, 2021-12-22.

[36] https://opensciences.org/about/manifesto-for-a-post-materialist-science

Made in the USA
Las Vegas, NV
30 October 2022

58443726R00105